J. Murray Mitchell

Foreign Missions of the Protestant Churches

Their State and Prospects

J. Murray Mitchell

Foreign Missions of the Protestant Churches
Their State and Prospects

ISBN/EAN: 9783337077327

Printed in Europe, USA, Canada, Australia, Japan

Cover: Foto ©Lupo / pixelio.de

More available books at **www.hansebooks.com**

FOREIGN MISSIONS

OF THE

PROTESTANT CHURCHES:

THEIR STATE AND PROSPECTS.

BY

J. MURRAY MITCHELL, M.A., LL.D.

TORONTO, CANADA:
TORONTO WILLARD TRACT DEPÔT,
CORNER YOUNGE AND TEMPERANCE STREETS.
1888.

PREFACE.

The following pages have been written under the impression that it is desirable at present to take a wide, general view of the field of Missions, and to present the great subject in a form short and simple enough to interest those to whom it may not be familiar.

Many even of the friends of Missions know little of the work, unless as done in connection with their own Church or Society. On many accounts this is to be regretted. For one thing, it is needful that there be in the future more of union and co-operation in Missionary effort than has hitherto been attained, or perhaps by some even thought of as desirable.

The main difficulty in drawing up the little book

has been in the necessity of compressing abundant materials into so limited a space.

Such as they are, the following pages, if but graciously owned of Him, "without whom nothing is strong, nothing is holy," may, it is hoped, be of some service in stimulating zeal and furthering united action on behalf of the turning of the Pagan nations from darkness unto light.

CONTENTS.

CHAP.		PAGE
I.	Introductory	1
II.	What the Missions have Done	12
III.	State of the Chief Pagan Religions	32
	Animism, etc.	32
	Zoroastrianism	33
	Buddhism	35
	Hinduism	40
	Mohammadanism	43
IV.	Modes of Missionary Action	61
	Bible Distribution	63
	Preaching	64
	Translation and Literary Work	65
	Schools	66
	Medical Missions	69
V.	What Next	74
	Enlargement of Effort Necessary	74
	How to Awaken Missionary Zeal	76

CONTENTS.

CHAP.
    Volunteer Missionaries
    Union and Co-operation
    Division of the Field
VI. Conclusion

APPENDIX.

A. Rise of Missionary Zeal since the Reformation
B. Indian Missionary Statistics
C. British Contributions to Foreign Mission Work
D. Present State of Educated Hindus
E. Mohammadan Intemperance
F. Creeds and Confessions in Mission Churches
G. Comparative Progress of Religions in India

Index

PROTESTANT FOREIGN MISSIONS.

I.

INTRODUCTORY.

I do not wait to prove—I simply assert what will, I trust, be on all hands admitted to be true—that the missionary spirit pervades the Word of God from Genesis to Revelation. The promise to Abraham was this: "In thee and in thy seed shall all the families of the earth be blessed." The prophets of Israel delighted to catch from afar the radiance of the coming glory. They rejoiced to declare that "the mountain of the Lord's house" should be "established in the top of the mountains," and that "all nations should flow unto it." Let Israel arise and shine; let her so shine that "the Gentiles might come to her light, and kings to the brightness of her rising." Nor was this desire extinguished in the breast of believing Jews even by the terrible persecutions to which, in later days, they were subjected by heathen oppressors. We note all the ardour of Isaiah in the words of the aged Simeon, when he hails in the infant Saviour "a light to lighten the Gentiles" as well as the glory of the people of Israel.

Our Blessed Master was Himself "sent only to the lost sheep of the house of Israel;" and Divine wisdom is traceable in the restriction. But all through the Gospel narrative there are affecting indications of what was deep in His mind and heart, in reference to the heathen nations. Let one quotation suffice. "Other sheep I have," said the Good Shepherd, "which are not of this fold; them also I must bring, and they shall hear My voice: and there shall be one flock,[1] one shepherd." The word *must* arrests attention. Why *must* He bring them? What necessity could be laid on Him who "worketh all things after the counsel of His own will"? Did it not lie both in the high decree of God, and in the strong compulsion of redeeming love, of which, indeed, the decree itself was but the expression? Even so felt the Apostles. Paul exulted in the thought of the everlasting Gospel as "made known to all nations for the obedience of faith." So doubtless felt the whole collective Church. Nor did the missionary spirit speedily pass away; the evangelising of the nations was in multitudes a

[1] So in the Greek.

passion, to all an admitted obligation; and this was the case through the Apostolic age and long afterwards. "*Every man a missionary*" may be said to have been the motto of the early Church.

As we come later down, we see a beautiful manifestation of evangelistic zeal on the part of the Nestorian Christians. The representatives of this once-flourishing body are found in Urumiah and among the mountains of Kurdistan; but they are few and feeble in comparison with what they formerly were; and, until of late, they have been sorely harassed by the Mohammadans around them.[1] The Nestorians were once a noble missionary Church. They influenced Arabia as well as Persia. They penetrated far eastward into Tartary, and, through Tartary, into China. The Syrian Church of Malabar in Southern India was established,[2] or at least greatly extended, by their labours. Their efforts to spread the Gospel were continued for nearly a thousand years. The vigour with which these were carried on has extorted the admiration even of Gibbon. "The zeal of the Nestorians," he tells us, "over-

---

[1] They were terribly wasted by the sword of Timur. We regret to have to add, in the words of Layard, that "the machinations and violence of the Popish emissaries against them would scarcely be credited."

[2] It is still a question whether the Apostle Thomas preached in India. That he did so is a very old tradition. *Parthia Matthæum complectitur, India Thomam*, said Paulinus of Nola (born A.D. 353).

leaped the limits which had confined the ambition and curiosity both of the Greeks and Romans. The missionaries of Balkh and Samarcand followed without fear the footsteps of the roving Tartar, and insinuated themselves into the camps in the valleys of the Imaus and on the banks of the Selinga."[1]

In Europe there was a manifestation of evangelistic ardour no less remarkable, and in our own islands too. The fire burnt with a bright and steady flame for at least four centuries. Columba came from Ireland to Iona in 543; and thenceforward, from that centre and from Ireland itself, the Celtic missionaries carried the tidings of salvation over the North of Scotland, the North of England, and a large part of Europe.[2] It has been well said that "the ardent nature of the Scot,[3] which kindled with burning zeal at the touch of the new faith, was only to be satisfied with perpetual propagandism." The share which Iona bore in this great work is especially remarkable. That insignificant island in the storm-vexed Hebrides, when once Columba had planted his Missionary College on

---

[1] Chap. xlvii.

[2] They spread themselves over England, France, Germany, Switzerland, and Italy, from the Mediterranean to Iceland. See Anderson's "Scotland in Early Christian Times," p. 162.

[3] We must remember that the name *Scots* was not given to the inhabitants of North Britain exclusively before the twelfth century.

its shores, became, in Dr. Johnson's well-known words, "illustrious"—"the luminary of the Caledonian regions;" or, in the still stronger language of Wordsworth, "the glory of the West." Nor must we overlook the important work of evangelisation carried on by the Cymri or Welsh, especially from Bangor as a centre, in the sixth century.[1] Thereafter, in our islands, evangelistic zeal never rose so high; and when the Saxon race was converted to Christianity, it gradually died out.[2]

It must be sorrowfully admitted that little or no zeal for the conversion of the heathen was evinced by the chief leaders of the Reformation. This may well surprise us, seeing that Luther, Melanchthon, Calvin, and others were large-minded and large-hearted men. How can we account for it? We must not forget what a tremendous battle they had to fight—a battle for imperilled truth, a battle for very existence; and let this consideration go for what it may be worth. Erasmus, alone of the

---

[1] Wales sent missionaries to Ireland and Brittany. See article on the Keltic Church in Schaff's Encyclopædia.

[2] The story of the conversion of Europe has the charm of a most interesting personal element in it when studied in connection with the lives of the following truly remarkable men:—Ulphilas, among the Goths, 4th century; Patrick, "the Apostle of Ireland," probably in the end of the 4th; Martin of Tours, in Gaul, 5th; Columba, 6th; Columbanus, 7th; Boniface, in Germany, 8th; Cyril and Methodius, among the Slavs, 9th; Anschar (one of the noblest of men), among the Scandinavians, 9th.

great men belonging to the Reformation era, contended for the evangelisation of the heathen nations; and he pleaded that this should be conducted on Scriptural principles, as distinct from the methods which were generally employed by Rome.[1]

The reader will find in Appendix A. a pretty full statement of the gradual increase of missionary zeal from the Reformation to near the end of last century. It is too long to be inserted here.

The year 1786 affords a new starting-point in mission history. In that year William Carey astonished a number of ministers of the Gospel by asking whether the command to preach the Gospel was not still binding on the Church of Christ. The devoted man persevered in his pleading, in spite of coldness and even opposition. In 1792 he preached a sermon which led to the foundation, on 2nd October of the same year, of the Baptist Missionary Society. Carey proceeded to Bengal in 1793.

The London Missionary Society dates from 1795. It was a broadly catholic institution, supported by members of all Protestant Churches. Its establishment gave an immense impulse to missions all over England and Scotland.

The Scottish Missionary Society was formed in 1796; the Netherlands Society in 1797; the

---

[1] In his *Ecclesiastes, sive de ratione concionandi*.

Church Missionary Society in 1799, though it assumed this specific designation only in 1812. The American Board of Commissioners for Foreign Missions was formed in 1810.

We cannot attempt to enumerate the societies which have come into existence in the course of the present century. The movement in favour of evangelising the nations, which was slow at first, has gone on with accelerated speed up to the present day. Thus there were, fifty years ago—

In Great Britain	10 Societies.
In the United States	7 „
On the Continent	10 „
	27 „

The number now is at least as high as the following estimate :—

In Great Britain and the Colonies .	25 Societies.
In the United States	39 „
On the Continent	40 „
	104 „

Nor is this list by any means complete. New Societies, small perhaps, but far from unimportant, are continually springing up.[1]

It is painful to think that for a long time many professed Christians were opposed to missions, and

[1] The *Quarterly Review* for July 1886 estimates all the Missionary Societies as not fewer than 146.

levelled against them the shafts both of argument and ridicule. Conspicuous among the mockers was Sidney Smith, who sneered at Carey as "a consecrated cobbler;" but it ought not to be forgotten that, in later days, he referred to his attacks on the Serampore missionaries as having been "absurdity, unadulterated and pure." The feeling in favour of missions has gone on increasing. A sarcastic fling at missionaries, or at speeches on missionary platforms, is still indulged in from time to time, and occasionally even a theologian, like the late Beck of Tübingen, may revert to Luther's position; but, speaking generally, we may say that serious argument against evangelistic effort has almost ceased. The practical results already realised compel the attention of the world. Fuller examination has dispelled the belief in the virtues once supposed to pertain to "the noble savage;" and few have the hardihood to deny that to turn cannibals even into "psalm-singing Methodists" is, on the whole, a gain to civilisation and humanity. It is right to mention that no one ever spoke more warmly of the results of missionary labour among degraded races than did Charles Darwin. "The missionary's teaching," said he, "is like an enchanter's wand." He alluded to what he had himself witnessed in the Southern Pacific.[1]

---

[1] Darwin was, to the last, a supporter of missions on the ground of

INTRODUCTORY.

Before proceeding farther, it is needful to mention that this paper will not treat of missions to the Jews. Assuredly we do not overlook the exceeding importance of these; but any satisfactory statement regarding them would extend this tractate far beyond its prescribed limits. Let it suffice to say, that the results of evangelistic work among the descendants of Israel have been by no means inconsiderable. The number of professed converts to Christianity is from 1000 to 1500 annually; and many, probably most, of these belong to the educated class. Recent movements among the Jews in South-Eastern Europe have been most remarkable, most encouraging; especially that in Bessarabia, with which the name of Joseph Rabinowich is associated. Rabbi Lichtenstein, near Buda-Pesth, seems also exerting a great influence for good. Movements on a grand scale may be at hand. It seems impossible to feel too intensely, or to hope too much, in regard to the changes in Jewish feeling which we witness at this hour. And "what shall the receiving of them be but life from the dead?"

philanthropy and civilisation. He had once had a very bad opinion of the inhabitants of Tierra del Fuego, deeming them utterly incorrigible. But he admitted and admired the wonderful success of the "South American Missionary Society" among these savages. He wrote, "It is most wonderful, and it shames me, as I always prophesied failure. It is a grand success. I shall feel proud if your committee think fit to elect me an honorary member of your Society."

We must also omit the very important work which is carried on by several Societies, chiefly American, among the Eastern Christians—Churches so venerable, yet in many respects so sorely fallen. The Nestorians; the Armenians; the Jacobite Syrians, and the Syrian Christians in Southern India (originally Nestorian); the Copts and Abyssinians; the members (belonging to various nationalities) of the Greek Church—among all of these there is a large amount of labour now carried on. The results have been especially conspicuous among the Nestorians, the Armenians, the Syrians in India, and the Copts. We may add the Bulgarians (who are members of the Greek Church); and in so far as Bulgaria has a national life, it owes that life to the Christian institution called Robert College, on the Bosphorus.[1]

[1] Dr. Claudius Buchanan by his "Christian Researches," published early in this century, awakened a deep interest regarding the Syrians in India. The Rev. W. Jowett, a few years later (1815), proceeded on a mission of inquiry to the Eastern Churches, and published a volume of "Researches" which is still useful. In 1821 Pliny Fisk and Levi Parsons proceeded to Palestine. Smith and Dwight went out in 1826 to investigate the condition of the Churches in Asia Minor. Gobat and Kugler proceeded to Abyssinia in 1829. Goodall began work in Constantinople in 1831. In 1833 Perkins did so among the Nestorians in Urumiah. In 1854 the United Presbyterians of America began work among the Copts. There is an impression in some quarters that the American Presbyterians and Congregationalists have gone forth with the express desire of "disintegrating" the Oriental Churches, or, as the Archbishop of Canterbury puts it, "to incorporate and obliterate ancient

INTRODUCTORY.

We also pass over the work carried on in Romanist countries, such as France, Italy, Spain, Portugal, and Mexico.

Churches." In this respect his Grace classes them with the Roman Catholics (see "The Seven Gifts," p. 215). Dr. Benson has been misinformed. Our American brethren do precisely what the Church Missionary Society does among the Syrians in Southern India, and what, in connection with the present Bishop of Jerusalem, the Archbishop has expressed his own approval of.

II.

WHAT THE MISSIONS HAVE DONE.

Referring those who desire fuller statistics to the notes in the Appendix, we here content ourselves with the following numerical statements as to the results of missionary labour.

The population of the world is probably above fourteen hundred millions. The nominally Christian part of this number is above four hundred millions. Thus the non-Christian portion of the human race, in round numbers, is a thousand millions. The ratio of professing Christians to non-Christians is as one to two and a half. Even if every professing Christian were a true Christian, the fact that, of the hundred sheep which the Good Shepherd claims as His own, more than seventy have wandered far from Him, would be full of solemn significance. And yet how quietly we take it! O Church of the Living God! where is thy zeal for the honour of thy Redeemer? where is thy pity for perishing humanity?

WHAT THE MISSIONS HAVE DONE.

The number of heathen in the present day must be much larger than it was when Jesus Christ issued the great command, "Preach the Gospel to every creature." Farther, the population of the globe is continually increasing. During the century that has elapsed since Carey's earnest appeal was made, at least two hundred millions, in all probability, have been added to the Pagan population of the world.[1]

Assuredly we have no desire to lessen the impression which facts like these are fitted to produce on every Christian heart. Yet there is a way of stating them which, though not erroneous, is misleading, because it is imperfect. Thus, as the number of converts from heathenism during the last hundred years can hardly be estimated as above three millions, a saddening contrast has often been drawn between the rapid growth of heathenism, and the slow progress of the Gospel in our day. Let us try, then, to look at the question all round.

The population of the globe is continually increasing, but the *proportional* increase is far higher in Christian than in heathen countries. We have no very reliable statistics, but we may roughly calculate the *actual* increase in Christendom during the last century to have been to that in Heathendom

[1] Very different estimates of the increase have been given. We believe it probably exceeds the number here stated.

as one to one and a half. For every ten millions added to Christendom there have been fully fifteen millions added to Heathendom. But the *proportional* increase has been very different; probably it has been twice as great in Christendom as in Heathendom. Before the end of this century the *actual* increase in the former will, in all likelihood, equal that in the latter; and thereafter it will shoot more and more ahead of it.

It is, of course, very easy to over-estimate the importance of this growth of nominal Christianity; and good men will sorrowfully exclaim, "Alas for the Christianity of Christendom!" But it is also possible to *under*-estimate the importance of this steady increase of professors of the Christian faith. Anyway, it is a fact; and it is so in spite of the growth, in certain quarters, of agnosticism, "esoteric Buddhism," and other forms of indifferentism and unbelief.

Farther, it is easy to slide into an extravagant statement of the rapidity with which the Gospel spread in the Apostolic period; and we must be on our guard against this. We have been told that, as soon as the silver trump of the Gospel sounded abroad, "the statue of every false god tottered to its base, the priest fled from his falling shrine, and the heathen oracles became dumb for ever." This is tolerable as rhetoric, but intolerable as history.

What was the number of professing Christians at the end of the first century? The highest possible estimate would be half a million of souls, but probably it was much less.[1] At the conversion of Constantine in the fourth century, the Christian population of the world probably did not exceed six millions. During the first centuries Christianity increased, but Paganism increased far more rapidly. That circumstance, however, was no discouragement to the Apostles and their fellow-labourers or successors. They knew that, though the battle might be sore, the victory was sure.

Instead of being discouraged because the number of converts from heathenism has, during the century, amounted only to three millions, we may well be astonished that the number is so large. Let us explain. When asked what is doing in the mission-field, we answer: In one point of view little; in another, much. On the part of man, very little in comparison with what ought to have been done; but considering how little man has done, very much on the part of God. Most righteously might the Lord have "withdrawn Himself to the uttermost part of heaven," and there "covered Himself with a cloud, that our prayer should not pass through." Most righteously might He have withheld His blessing from our faltering, almost faith-

---

[1] Dr. Warneck makes it only 200,000.

less doings, and waited until His people should have come forward with some measure of that holy consecration which befits the men who are summoned forth as auxiliaries of Heaven. But, in His boundless mercy, He has not so waited. He largely blesses our initial efforts. Not a single blow—not the feeblest—does He allow to be struck in vain. One thing, then, has been proved abundantly. Through the grace of God, the Gospel is as mighty now to the pulling down of strongholds as it was of old. "The foolishness of the preaching" effects the same transformation still, when it comes from the stammering tongues of ordinary men, as when it flowed in heaven-taught, burning accents from the lips of Paul or John. Men of all religions, fetish-worshippers, demon-worshippers, monotheistic Moslem, polytheistic Chinese, and pantheistic Brahmans, the civilised Japanese, and the cannibal of New Guinea, all confess its resistless sway; and wheresoever and whensoever

> "The holy words diffusing balm,
> The message of the sacrifice,
> Are heard within the caves of ice,
> Or preached beneath the cocoa-palm,"

there and then the same unvarying result is witnessed. We say it is witnessed in every case, though not everywhere and always to the same extent. Some races and some religions yield to the sway of the Gospel more readily than others; but no race, no faith, is wholly proof against its unearthly power. No race, no faith, can long resist its calm, majestic, and continuous march. It speaks; heart and conscience are aroused, and ere long respond. It proclaims, as with the voice of a trumpet,

> "Truths which wake,
> To perish never."

And be it remembered, that it is no altered or diluted Gospel which has thus been proved invincible. Some men would fain persuade us that, in these enlightened days, when physical science scarcely tolerates the idea of miracle, and ethics looks shy on Atonement, we must adapt our doctrine to the spirit of the age, proclaiming Christ as only an exalted teacher,—a wiser Buddha, or a nobler Socrates. The missionaries will reply that the change is no more needful than it is for them possible. They have preached without reserve the dogmas of the incarnation, the atoning death, and the resurrection of the Lord Jesus; and they have found that the exhibition of Christ crucified is "the power of God unto salvation to every one who believeth." Why should they change their voice? Let those who are in love with an emasculated Gospel try for themselves its efficacy. Why are

B

they so slow in doing it? But the Missionaries, for every reason, will still unfurl the old banner, and ply their proved war-weapons of victory.

And this is not all. For certainly the great pioneers of modern missions were, in Lord Shaftesbury's phrase, "Evangelicals of the Evangelicals." Eliot, the Mayhews, and Brainerd in New England were Puritans. Ziegenbalg and the admirable men who succeeded him in South India were Pietists. So, in a pre-eminent degree, were the Moravians— men, let us frankly grant, of no intellectual culture and no breadth of view, delighting in hymns which often conveyed the truth in language painfully rude. But they clung, as with a death-grip, to the teaching of the Scripture regarding sin, and salvation, and Christ crucified; and thus the earthen vessels contained heavenly treasure, and the excellency of the power which accompanied them was seen to be of God, and not of man.[1]

But it will be said that as yet we have spoken only of numerical results, and that we must weigh, as well as count, the accessions to the faith. By all means. What, then, speaking generally, is the character of the converts? We naturally first

---

[1] We speak of *pioneers*. Hans Egede, however, was, of course, a Lutheran Churchman. In more recent times, some who may be designated High Churchmen, like Bishops Mackenzie, Selwyn, and Steere, have nobly distinguished themselves in the mission-field.

compare it with the character they bore as Pagans. As we were preparing to discuss this subject, a document from India came into our hands, which gave the following important statement regarding the proportions of convicts and criminals among the professors of the three great religions of Southern India:—

"There is one criminal among 447 Hindus.
   ,,   ,,   ,,   728 Musulmans.
   ,,   ,,   ,,   2500 Christians." [1]

These figures must be, on the whole, fairly accurate; and if so, they clearly show the purifying influence of the Gospel in comparatively civilised lands. We do not venture to generalise, and say that the ratios would be precisely the same elsewhere; but that everywhere the Gospel purifies and elevates is beyond dispute. With regard to the more degraded races, let it suffice to quote again from a writer whose testimony will not be called in question by the most prejudiced scorner of missions: —" The march of improvement consequent upon the introduction of Christianity throughout the South Seas probably stands by itself in the records of history." " Within twenty years, human sacrifices, the power of an idolatrous priesthood, profligacy unparalleled in any other part of the world, infanticide, bloody wars—not sparing women and children, all

[1] *Madras Weekly Mail*, January 26, 1887.

these have been abolished, and dishonesty, intemperance, and licentiousness greatly reduced by the introduction of Christianity."[1] True, tares are mingled with the wheat. When I put a question on this subject to an experienced missionary soon after my arrival in India, he said, "We get the best and the worst." In India educated converts, in that day of small things, were very few; but now, for many years, they have been numerous. Accessions of the best—the best both spiritually and intellectually—have long been multiplying.

The change effected by the Gospel is perhaps, as was to be expected, everywhere most manifest among the women. In Southern India, for example, you can tell whether the village is largely Christianised by the appearance of the women at the well. Their dress is more seemly. Their very look is different. Nearly every Hindu woman has a careworn, anxious face; as if the battle of life tried her sore. The Christian woman has a far more peaceful expression. Of course all Christian girls are more or less educated, and this gives them an immense advantage over their Hindu sisters. The Christian women of India, when carefully trained, reveal in their characters as much of true womanhood and purity, and faith and love, even as their favoured sisters in Europe or America.

[1] Darwin's "Voyage of the Beagle," pp. 505, 414 (Edit. 1860).

I am convinced that the average character of converts in India—and what is true of India in this respect is true of the mission-field generally—is more than equal to the average character of professing Christians at home. And if this be true, is it not a wonderful truth? Let us think what long centuries of Pagan belief and rites have done to debase the character. Let us then recollect what centuries of Christian education have accomplished in purifying and elevating the mind and heart of Europe. Take Scotland, for example. There an excellent system of national education has been moulding the character of the whole people since the days of Knox. It seems almost incredible that converts and their children in Heathendom should stand a moment's comparison with the inhabitants of Christendom; and yet we fearlessly challenge the comparison.

Still it is said that, at all events, the character of the converts lacks solidity and strength; emotion, rather than conscience, rules; they are always soft and weak. One word about the supposed weakness. Before the great mutiny of 1857 in India, if missionaries had been asked what would be the effect of persecution on the Native Church, they would probably have expressed but little hope that the converts would aspire to the crown of martyrdom. Well, the terrible convulsion came, but the Native

Church clung faithfully to Christ. Not a few meekly endured great suffering, and some calmly died the martyr's death.[1] But when we speak of martyrdom, we cannot but remember with tearful admiration the heroic constancy of the martyrs of Madagascar, or, more recently still, of the young African converts—mere boys, several of them—that lately met a most cruel death on the shores of the Victoria Nyanza. Is there in the martyrology of the Church a more thrilling story? And if few—though not so few as is supposed—have of late years been called with this highest of callings, yet cases of purest self-sacrifice, of sore suffering meekly borne for Christ, are of continual occurrence. The Church knows little of these confessors; the world generally knows nothing. Nevertheless their record is on high. No; "the ancient spirit is not dead;" the Spirit of God still works in the heart of converts as He wrought of old; and what Milton calls "the unresistible might of weakness" is no less conspicuous now than it was in the purest days of infant Christianity. *Laus Deo!*[2]

---

[1] "Many of them perished; they were blown from guns; they were cut down by the sword; they died of starvation in their wanderings. Yet when we came to collect after the mutiny and compare notes, so far as we could discover, only two had consented to become Mohammadans through fear."—*Leupolt, at Liverpool Conference*, 1860.

[2] "Above all, the Christian character of the native converts is

One important result of missions is the effect on those who are still without the pale of the Church —not communicants, nor even baptized. It has been said that in India, for every one actually baptized there are ten convinced. Multitudes, of young men especially, have had their minds more or less enlightened by Christian truth, who, though afraid to profess their faith openly, strive to make a religion of morality, accepting the teachings of the Gospel as their guide. Very affecting cases occur from time to time of men proclaiming on their death-bed the faith which they had through life concealed, and then craving the administration of baptism. In the West, men are slow to comprehend this hesitation to come out and be separate, and they are strong in condemning it. We by no means justify it; but we understand it. Let us remember that in India baptism, as a rule, entails expulsion from home—a terrible calamity to a Hindu—and expulsion also from caste, which is equivalent to civil death. Then, the tears of father and mother, and the entreaty that the baptism may be at least deferred, are too powerful for many to resist, even when of themselves they are quite ready to profess

assuming greater depth and earnestness, and their share in evangelistic work is steadily increasing in value as well as in amount."
—*Missionary Herald (American)*, November 1887.

"Never was the outlook more hopeful in the Heathen and Mohammadan world."—*Report of C. M. S.*, 1886-87.

Christ openly. In many who thus hesitate the first love seems to pass away, and they never do actually enter the Church of Christ. Some may go so far as to practise again, without having faith in them, the rites of Hinduism. It is a strange and sad state of things, no doubt; yet it cannot greatly surprise us. It is, however, but temporary; and already cases occur—and will certainly do so with increasing frequency—in which the Christian son or daughter is allowed to remain in the family without being solicited to join in any idolatrous rites.[1]

Every missionary who has been several years in India is aware of a great change in the feeling of the people generally towards Christians and Christianity. There *was* a feeling almost of horror when a conversion had taken place. It was no doubt traceable, in part, to the difference of Eastern and Western customs; the people wondered at our habits, and disliked them.[2] That one of their

---

[1] One of the most recent testimonies to the spread of Christian ideas, and we may say feelings, is given by Sir Charles Aitchison as follows:—" Missionary teaching and Christian literature are leavening native opinion, especially among the Hindus, in a way and to an extent quite startling to those who take a little personal trouble to investigate the facts." He then mentions the case of one of the ruling powers of India, who probably never saw a missionary, but who has a Sanskrit Bible, which he carefully reads, and who " prays to Christ every day for the pardon of his sins." We believe that cases of this kind are multiplying.

[2] Especially the eating of beef—the cow being sacred, and, in fact, a goddess.

number should unite himself with those strange, masterful, disagreeable foreigners, was dreadful; they felt much as we should do if a son of ours went—as the hero of "Locksley Hall" threatened to do—and wedded "some savage woman." But although the dislike of European habits still exists, the Hindus see in the native churches rising up around them, that their people who become Christians can remain, in language and dress and mode of living, all they were before.

But along with this there is a rapidly growing conviction that, apart from outlandish habits, Christianity is a pure and good religion. People are learning to distinguish between profession and practice, between true and false Christians. They believe that the Gospel must conquer in the end, and will often admit that it ought to conquer. In all parts of the country missionaries are thus addressed by men of all classes, except, perhaps, Brahmans and Mohammadans: "*We* are too old to become Christians, but our children or grandchildren will be with you." This anticipation arises, in part, from the important fact that everywhere in India the Christian communities are increasing in intelligence,[1] in

---

[1] We confess our surprise at the rapidity of the rise in intelligence. Thus at a late B.A. examination in the Madras University, the percentage of the Brahmans who passed was thirty-six, and that of the Christians thirty-seven. Undoubtedly the Brahmans are a highly intellectual class, and we were not prepared to

position, and in influence. Even the Karens in Burmah, who were simply savages before their conversion, are steadily rising, and must gradually take precedence of the Burmese who may continue Buddhists.

And further, Christianity powerfully affects many who have no love for it as an aggressive system, and would fain withstand its progress. Of course, all the moral teachings of the Gospel, and all that part of it which Butler calls "a republication of Natural Religion,"—command the assent of educated men. The effect of these teachings extends far beyond the circle of the baptized. The educated exclaim, "All that is true, but our books inculcate it as really as the Bible does." And hence eclecticism,—an eager attempt to cull golden sentences from Hindu books and bracket them as equals with Christian maxims.[1] The most remarkable instance of this

find the Christians already equalling or excelling them in their chief characteristic.—See *Madras Weekly Mail*, January 1887.

[1] We by no means charge the men who thus recast Hinduism with conscious deception. Doubtless, in many cases, they think they do find what they wish to find. Nor need we be surprised that there is an earnest desire to prove Hinduism, at least in some things, more enlightened than the Gospel. Thus we see it stated that the Hon. G. R. Ranade, one of the best-educated Hindus in Western India, extols Hinduism on account of its "indefiniteness and tolerance." Indefinite it is, to any extent, in its beliefs, but in its rules and restrictions as to caste it is immensely and sternly definite. And as for tolerance, a breach of caste-rules simply involves excommunication, which is equivalent, we have said, to

strong tendency is now seen in the proceedings of what is called the Arya Samaj. The Samaj makes a desperate effort to prove that the early hymns of India are monotheistic, and that the many deities invoked are all names of one great Being,—polytheism, pantheism, and idolatry being thus all discarded.[1] It is a striking spectacle. No doubt there mingles in it a large amount of national and ancestral pride. It is a most difficult task to convince a Hindu that ancient India was not at once the wisest and the greatest of nations;—and that God should have spoken to men through Jewish prophets rather than by Aryan Rishis, is to him an almost impossible belief. But the fact is as we have stated it; and it has a hopeful side. One after another the great truths of Revelation are admitted; and then they are found, or fancied, to be already imbedded in Vedic hymns, whose true meaning, we are told, has only now been brought to light. Men are thus reading Christianity into Hinduism, as Sir Edwin Arnold, in his very poetical, very unhistorical "Light of Asia," has read it,

---

civil death. Mr. Ranade should have known better. But the truth is, that educated Hindus are driven to strange shifts in defending the indefensible.

[1] In their worship, as conducted in London, there is much singing of Christian hymns, but the name of Christ seems systematically excluded. The original hymns are vehemently patriotic. The ancient glory of India is extravagantly insisted on.

to a large extent, into Buddhism; and in Japan itself, a distinguished leader of the Shinshiu sect assured us that, with him and many others, Amida Buddha occupied almost exactly the position which Christ does in Christianity, and that even the doctrine of the Atonement was accepted by them. All this demonstrates the deep impression which the teachings of Christianity are making on the systems of faith with which it comes in contact, and it is clearly indicative of its final triumph. It is very similar to what occurred in the early days of Christianity. The Gnostic and philosophic systems that then contended with the Gospel, and did so most successfully when they stole their weapons from it, were strange comminglings of truth and error; and from the outset they were doomed to pass away and perish, or else be gradually absorbed in the Church Catholic.

The immense multitude of minds to which the great truths of the Gospel are now steadily presented may be best conceived when we remember, that the Holy Scriptures are circulated in more than two hundred and eighty languages, and that the number of versions is steadily increasing. The important work of translation has been executed mainly by missionaries. Tracts and books have also been composed in nearly as large a number of dialects. At first the task of translating the Holy Scriptures and laying the foundations of a Christian literature fell naturally to the foreign missionaries. But in the older missions, for a good many years past, the Native Christians have taken a large and increasing share in this very important work.[1]

We must not forget the very large amount of work performed by the missions, which, although not directly evangelistic, is yet decidedly a *præparatio evangelica*,—such as the preparation of grammars and dictionaries, and the investigation of native literature, when any such exists. We add geographical exploration, in which many missionaries besides Livingstone have rendered very valuable service. They have also largely contributed to our knowledge of the botany, zoology, &c., &c., of the various regions in which their lot has been cast.

We might say much of the effect of missions in extending commerce. Moffat, speaking of the commencement of his labours in South Africa, observes: "Our efforts were the precursors of a mighty change,

[1] We have one remarkable example of this in the case of the Rev. Baba Padmanji, an alumnus of the Free Church Institution, Bombay. He has devoted nearly all his life to the work of Christian literature; and he is the author of more than fifty publications, some of them works of considerable size, and all of them of value.

destined to sweep away the filth and customs of former generations, and to open up numberless channels for British commerce, which, but for the Gospel, might have remained for ever closed."

Such is a brief statement of the results of missionary labour in the foreign field. No one will venture to call them small or unimportant. With all humility, we aver that the men have worked nobly, and that the blessing with which God has honoured their exertions has been great. The Church of Christ is bound to render thanks with her whole heart and soul, because of the Lord's overflowing goodness in accepting with such gracious acknowledgment the poor service rendered by His people.

We once climbed to a mountain summit in the Western Ghāts in search of the source of the Godavari, one of the greater rivers of India. We came at last to a spot where some drops were trickling, but so few that, for two or three seconds, we held the whole stream in the hollow of our hand. We then with the eye traced the descending rill, and saw it gradually broaden. We followed it in thought as it flowed eastward towards the Bay of Bengal, while, "with pomp of waters unwithstood," it expanded and expanded, until it became capable of fertilising ten thousands of acres that would otherwise have remained for ever barren.

Even so have we sought to trace, from its almost imperceptible commencement, the stream of modern missionary effort. What a blessed change since the admirable Von Welz, two centuries ago, was striving with a breaking heart, and vainly striving, to arouse the slumbering Churches of Germany to the necessity of obeying the great commission! Aye, what a change since, only a century ago, Carey was ridiculed as "a miserable enthusiast," and told by divines of high repute that, unless the Pentecostal gift of tongues were renewed, it was absurd to attempt to evangelise the nations! How vast the change both at home and abroad! And yet all that we yet witness is but the commencement. For the blessed stream rolls on, and will roll on, ever broadening and deepening as it flows,—causing "the wilderness and solitary place to be glad, and the desert to rejoice and blossom as the rose."

III.

STATE OF THE CHIEF PAGAN RELIGIONS.

It may, we trust, be of service for us to take a glance at the chief Pagan religions, and endeavour to estimate the amount of force which they possess in the conflict with Christianity.

ANIMISM, ETC.

The lowest forms of religion are those that prevail among savage races and those that are slightly nearer civilisation. These have been styled "polydemonistic, magical, tribal religions,"[1] and are frequently classed under the head of Animism, or the worship of spirits. Fetishism is distinguishable from this, but easily blends with it. These religions have been called polydemonistic rather than polytheistic, because the beings worshipped are almost universally malevolent, and the worship springs simply from fear, and is a deprecation of evil. They always run into sorcery and magic. They have hardly any

[1] So Professor Tiele calls them.

moral character. This unhappy creed is very extensively diffused. It rules in Africa, except where Mohammadanism or Christianity has expelled it. It prevails in Northern Asia, unless where Buddhism or Christianity to some extent counteracts it. It is in the South Seas, but there it is rapidly giving way before the Gospel. It cannot be called a system, it is so vague and shapeless; and before any definite form of religion it speedily succumbs.

But let us pass to higher creeds, and among these let us first notice

ZOROASTRIANISM.

The founder of this system is said by its professors to have been the famous Zoroaster. It was at one time widely extended, under the patronage of the kings of Persia, and aspired to become a universal creed. It now exists only in Persia and India. In Persia it is dying out, chiefly because crushed under the iron heel of Mohammadanism.[1] In Western India its followers, the Parsis, are a small but intelligent and influential body. As a race, they are energetic and practical. Western ideas and habits are steadily flowing in amongst them. In point of female education they have shot far ahead of the

---

[1] In October 1879 there were only 8499 Zoroastrians in Persia. In 1881 there were in all India only 85,397.

Hindus. Still, as yet, they cling with a pathetic fondness to the profession of Zoroastrianism. But the faith, as a faith, declines. It tends to resolve itself into simple monotheism, tinctured by the teachings of Christianity. The sacred book ascribed to Zoroaster, the Zend-Avesta, though not immoral, is but a shallow production, and cannot long satisfy the awakening mind of the Parsi community. The rites are both foolish and complex; some of them so coarse as to repel and disgust the younger generation. It is inconceivable that such a system should long continue to rule the mind of an active and intelligent race. Time was when Chosroes II. (called by the Parsis, Khosru Parviz) vowed that he would consent to no cessation of war against the Christians until "the religion of the Cross" had been overthrown and "the religion of the Sun" erected on its ruins. Vain boast! In the very land in which the proud words were uttered the religion of the Sun seems doomed to expire within a generation. In India it will survive somewhat longer, at least in name; but every conception on religion entertained by the Parsis is more and more affected by Christianity.[1] Conversions from Zoroastrianism in

[1] For example, the *dualism*, so characteristic of the original creed, has almost entirely passed away; and the relation between the good and evil principles, Hormazd and Ahriman (Oromasdes and Arimanes), is understood to be that which exists between God and Satan.

India have not been numerous, but they have been most satisfactory. We may now speak of

BUDDHISM.

Very erroneous statements are often made as to the extent of this system, if system it can be called, seeing that its diversities are exceedingly great. First, the population of China is considerably overstated, for it is probably under four hundred millions. Next it is quietly assumed that all the Chinese are Buddhists; but in truth every Chinaman holds a composite creed, of which, in many cases, the smallest ingredient is Buddhism. The educated and official classes profess themselves followers of Confucius, and as a rule would refuse to be designated Buddhists. All things considered, if we calculate the professors of Buddhism at three hundred millions, the estimate is decidedly a high one.

In most places Buddhism is content when it can hold its own.

In Northern Asia it blends with Shamanism, which is a form of Animism or spirit-worship, and in that case all that is best in Buddhism disappears.

In Japan, where it has branched out into eight

varieties, it is rapidly giving way before advancing Christianity. In that country the original faith was Shintoism—the feeblest, vaguest, and most colourless of religions. Buddhism, as a more definite system, was gradually displacing the ancient faith; but now both Buddhism and Shintoism are crumbling into ruins, and we seem "within measurable distance" of a national conversion to Christianity—we mean a national profession of it. There is some danger that the "Land of the Rising Sun," as Japan calls itself, may declare itself Christian prematurely. Influential public men are advocating this step on political grounds, believing that only thus will Japan be permitted to enter the sisterhood of civilised and Christian nations, and be treated as an equal by the proud peoples of the West. The change of feeling is truly marvellous. It is difficult to recall any nation or age in which equal progress has been made in an equal period of time. It was in 1853 that Commodore Perry, to the consternation of the Japanese, sailed into the Bay of Yeddo and induced them to open their country to intercourse with other nations. Public preaching has been possible only since 1873; and now the Christian community connected with Protestant missions alone is above 50,000. If Japan is not all professedly Christian by the end of this century—thirteen years hence—it seems at least certain that foreign missionaries will then no longer be required. Japanese Christians will themselves evangelise any portion of their countrymen that may still remain Pagan. Regarding the magnitude of the change that has already taken place, we content ourselves with quoting the words of a missionary at Kiyoto: "The half has not been told; it cannot be told. It must be seen and felt here on the ground." Other reforms accompany and aid the religious movement, even as they themselves have in large measure sprung out of it. The educational system, both in character and extent, reflects the highest credit on the Government. The schools even for women are numerous. Farther, it is almost certain that the exceedingly complicated characters in which the language has hitherto been written will be displaced by the Roman alphabet. English is greatly studied; it looks, indeed, as if it would gradually become a second national language.

One may not be able to witness all these rapid changes with unmingled satisfaction; for a nation cannot break abruptly with its past without running serious risk. The importation of the forms of Western civilisation, apart from the religion on which that civilisation is based, would be a very doubtful blessing. But happily, as we have seen, the Gospel is rapidly extending; while both the feeble Shintoism and the stronger Buddhism are as rapidly receding.

In China, Buddhism is not so visibly losing the measure of influence which it possesses. China has hitherto been eminently slow in moving. But these are days in which, as in those that ushered in the Christian era, the Ruler of the Universe is signally "shaking all nations;" and national pride, and policy, and tradition must bend to His sovereign will. The Chinese Government has of late [1] declared Christianity to be a good religion, and it undertakes to protect both the missionaries and the converts. Every change in such a country which is not positively for the worse is for the better; it familiarises the mind with the idea—so new to the Eastern world—of progress, of improvement. We therefore rejoice that telegraphs are spreading over China, and that railways are likely to follow. More important still,—the ancient classics, which have been the mainstay of the dominant Confucianism, and on a knowledge of which all promotion in the public service has depended, are about to sustain an unequal competition with the science of the West. Examinations in mathematics are already provided for, though not prescribed. The study of physical science will soon come, and must effect enormous

[1] In the autumn of 1886.

THE CHIEF PAGAN RELIGIONS. 39

changes. The throne of Confucius, we might almost say, begins to totter.

Forty years ago the Protestant Christians in China did not exceed three in number. Now the communicants are about 30,000; and the native Protestant community cannot be reckoned as less than 100,000. It doubles itself in about eight years.[1]

Tibet, with its fantastic form of Buddhism, Lamaism, has hitherto been all but inaccessible to evangelistic effort. The Moravians have had for a good many years one station whence they hoped to effect it, viz., Kyelang in Lahoul. There is now a second station on the borders of Tibet Proper, and a third has lately been opened at Leh, the capital of the Tibetan province of Ladak. The assault then on Lamaism has now fairly commenced.

In the southern countries of Ceylon, Burma, and Siam, Buddhism remains far nearer its original form than in the more northern countries of Asia. The mythology is less extravagant, the ritual less dazzling,

---

[1] In various parts of China there are races that are almost, or altogether, savage. Among these the inhabitants of the island of Formosa occupy an important place. Two missions labour in this island, those of the English Presbyterian Church and the Canada Presbyterian Church; and the blessing given to both has been very large.

—though Northern Buddhism, in several respects, responds to the cravings of the human soul better than the dreary creed of the south. Ceylon is a sacred land to Buddhists, especially those of the Southern school. Among other things, it boasts of possessing a tooth of Buddha, a relic deemed most precious, though certainly it never stood in a human jaw. Hence in Ceylon, Buddhism is tenacious of life. Yet the progress of the Gospel is encouraging.

In Siam the opposition is decidedly less and the prospect still more cheering.[1]

HINDUISM.

In the foregoing section we have referred, in several cases, for illustration, to this great system of belief. Our remarks at present may in consequence be all the briefer. Hinduism has often been classed as a non-missionary religion. Yet, in fact, it has continued to advance among the aboriginal races up to the present time. These accessions are not received into the proper Hindu community; they

---

[1] On the part of the Agnosticism of our day, there is a disposition to patronise Buddhism, if not to fraternise with it. How far is the alliance to extend? It was in Ceylon, we believe, that Bishop Heber asked a Buddhist priest, "Do you worship the gods?" and was startled by the reply, "No, the gods worship me." Our Agnostic friends, we presume, will draw the line before reaching that point, and, if they are wise, they will do it a good deal sooner.

hang on to it, so to speak; they are treated as without caste. They accept the degradation, and they think they are better than they were. Truly it was high time for missionaries to preach to the Kols, Santals, Khasias, and such simple tribes; for these are days of rapid innovation, even in conservative India, and, in one or two generations more, most of the aborigines would have been swallowed up in the *mare magnum* around them. A vague, shapeless demonology like theirs speedily gives way before a system with definite beliefs and rites. Their beliefs, however, are but little changed; only a few ceremonies are adopted. Happily, several missions are now energetically at work among these people, and in almost every case with very cheering results. This is true especially of the Kols, Santals, Khasias, and Garos. In Burma the change among the Karens has been still more rapid and complete.

But while gaining in this sense from the aborigines, Hinduism is engaged in a death-struggle with Christianity. We have already spoken of the way in which the *lucida tela diei*—the arrows of Gospel light—are piercing it through and through. Of course we do not assert that the only influence which tells on Hinduism is that of missions. Many things combine against it. Ours, as Sir Fitzjames Stephen says, is " a belligerent civilisation." British government, British law, education, railways, commerce—all conspire to overturn it. They infuse ideas entirely incompatible with those of the Shastras, and they necessitate ere long a change of institutions. This remark, indeed, applies to all non-Christian systems. They languish and gradually expire when exposed to the "fierce light" of modern thought and life. But Hinduism is vulnerable at every point—more so than most other creeds.

While the influences now referred to are mainly destructive, the Gospel destroys in order to reconstruct. Christianity is advancing in India; and, comparing one decade with another, it is doing so more and more rapidly. True, the advance has mainly been among the aborigines and the classes which, as we have said, "hang on" to Hinduism. Still there have been not a few cases, especially in Northern and Western India, of conversion among the higher and middle castes. Europeans may talk of the failure of missions; intelligent Hindus know better. They confess that, whatever may succeed it, Hinduism is doomed; or, if they maintain that it can live on, they mean a Hinduism which is not Hinduism. Doubtless the outer shell may remain for a time after the informing spirit shall have fled; but it too is mouldering away. We hardly anticipate its speedy destruction; we look for a steady, slow decay. Attempts will variously be made to reform it. We have spoken above of the Arya Samaj.[1] But, on the whole (so far as the masses are concerned), the battle will be between Hinduism proper and the Gospel.

It may be said that we are forgetting the philosophies of India—those systems of thought which ancient sages, with infinite refinements, so elaborately reasoned out. Well, these will always be interesting as studies in archæology; but, as Burnouf expressed it, it was to " the comprehension of the incomprehensible " that the Hindu philosophers " devoted all their faculties." To the sum of enduring thought they contributed simply nothing. The philosophies of India will therefore not prove any real obstacle to the progress of the Gospel among men who have received education in the European sense of the word.

MOHAMMADANISM.

In regard to the extent and progress of this great system there has recently been an animated, not to say a bitter, controversy. A good deal has been said which had better been left unsaid. Bold inferences have been drawn from very questionable

[1] The Brahma Samaj (except perhaps the moribund Adi Samaj) cannot well be called a *Hindu* system; the Hindu elements have been purged away almost entirely.

statistics. We trust we may be kept from exemplifying the rashness which we censure.[1]

Let us commence with the farthest East.

In *Japan* Islam hardly has a footing. In the large extent of the *Chinese Empire* it is found widely scattered, especially in the western provinces. Its adherents are about four millions. On the whole, it is quiet and unprogressive, and this mainly because in the western regions—Yunnan and Kashgar especially—its fiery zeal was, some years ago, quenched in blood. The same unrelenting cruelty with which Islam has generally been propagated was shown by the Chinese towards its rebellious professors.

In *Persia*, the suppression, or, to speak more accurately, the repression of that remarkable sect, the Bābis, has been as fiercely sanguinary as any-

[1] The Mohammadan population of the world is roughly estimated at 160 millions. A full third part of the whole is in India.

Islam is by no means a uniform system. Its diversities in belief and practice are many and great. The two grand divisions are the Sunni and the Shiah systems. These differ in many small and some very important points. For one thing, the Shiahs pay almost divine honour to Ali, the son-in-law of Mohammad. The stern and fanatical Wahabi system is mainly confined to Arabia.

The Shiah creed prevails in Persia; but Sufiism is still influential there, although the name may have fallen somewhat into disuse. Sufiism is a mystical philosophy, a species of Quietism, with a strong leaning to Pantheism, in which thoughtful, earnest minds, sick of the hard externalism of Islam, seek a refuge. Bābism has affinities to this system, with some leanings towards Christian thought, and much more love to Christians than to Moslem.

thing recorded in history. Fanaticism is not dead in Persia. Open preaching to Mohammadans is not yet possible. But religious inquiry goes on in secret; and, where the missionary cannot preach, the testimony of the Word of God is by no means ineffectual. We find a missionary in Persia lately saying that the Mohammadans there are "more and more accessible to evangelistic effort."

In *Arabia* it is usually supposed that the Gospel can be preached only at Aden and the neighbourhood; but recent inquiries [1] give a more encouraging idea of this important region. The population of Arabia may be from eight to ten millions. Three millions are under Turkish rule; the rest are independent. Under the Turks the proclamation of the Gospel would encounter the strongest opposition; but not so, probably, in Independent Arabia. The number of readers is considerable; and the circulation of the Scriptures would hardly be opposed, except under Turkish rule. Medical missions could do immense good. No doubt, when open conversions took place, there would be persecution, even among the independent tribes. But we must not think of Arabia as now closed against the Gospel.[2]

[1] Especially those conducted by General Haig.
[2] At Shaikh Othman, near Aden, but in British territory, the recent death of the Hon. Ion Keith-Falconer, a most accomplished and devoted man, has been a sad blow to the work in Arabia. But the mission which he so hopefully began will be energetically carried on by the Free Church of Scotland.

In *Egypt* there is much toleration, and the Egyptian authorities deserve credit for this; although the influence of the English and other foreigners may partly explain it. Conversions quietly take place from Islam from time to time. There have been more than sixty of these already.

In *North Africa*, viz., Morocco, Algeria, Tunis, Tripoli, and the Sahara, the Mohammadans are believed to number nearly sixteen millions. They are by no means inaccessible to evangelistic effort. Wherever missionaries go among them they are received with respect, almost with kindness.[1] It is sad to think what North Africa, once so highly civilised and flourishing, has become under the dominion of Islam; but let us not despair of its future.

Turkey.—Throughout all the Turkish Empire direct missionary labour among Mohammadans is at present almost impossible. About thirty years ago, and apparently as a result of the Crimean war, a very hopeful movement took place, especially in Constantinople. The Scriptures were freely sold in the streets, and largely purchased. There was much religious inquiry; people even of position flocked to the house of such converts as Selim Effendi, to hear him explain the Gospel. But from about 1864

[1] Report of Mildmay Conference of 1886, p. 28.

the authorities took the alarm, and ere long much was heard about a " new departure " of Islam, that is, a revival of Mohammadan zeal, which extended far beyond the boundaries of Turkey. Islam seemed to waken up to fresh life, being determined to resist, at all events, farther encroachments on its domain. Up to this hour the Turkish authorities are anxious to ignore the concessions of the Hatti Humayoon of 1856, even in spite of remonstrances from various quarters. Converts from Islam to Christianity are got rid of; and inquiries, though pressed by foreign ambassadors, are without result. Mission schools are closed; and if liberty be extorted to re-open them, yet Moslem children are forbidden to attend. Mohammadans are building mosques and opening schools throughout Asiatic Turkey with a zeal unknown for generations. The Sultan himself is earnest in this matter. All this is important. Islam in high quarters stands sternly on the defensive. Still in Turkey it is not progressive; and we presume it is as true now as it was when, more than fifty years ago, Lamartine used the memorable words, that Turkey is " perishing for want of Turks."

India.—There is a belief in some quarters that India is gradually becoming Mohammadan. Assuredly such is not the conviction which a somewhat lengthened experience in India has led us to form.[1] We sum up the results of that experience thus:—

1. Undoubtedly the antagonism between Islam and Hinduism is increasing. One of the great problems of British administration in India is how to keep Hindus and Mohammadans from flying at one another's throats. 2. Forcible conversions to Islam sometimes take place in Mohammadan states. 3. Women who have lost character and caste generally call themselves Musulmanis. 4. There has been from time to time, and there might be at any time, a rekindling of Moslem fanaticism in districts where Wahabi or Ferazi preachers make their rounds; a matter, no doubt, serious enough to demand the careful attention of Government. 5. We have also known one or two cases in which a zealous propagandist had been the occasion of the construction or reconstruction of mosques. 6. There is an influx into great commercial centres—such as Bombay—from Arabia, Persia, and other Mohammadan countries. 7. Further, Islam increases with the natural increase of population. 8. The Mohammadan *caste* is respectable; and there is a temptation to those who are in the lower strata of society to better their position by becoming Moslems. But

---

[1] We are glad to find our views as to the non-progressiveness of Islam in India are in accordance with those of Sir Alfred Lyall. See "Asiatic Studies," p. 111.

we have been surprised to see how little the temptation is yielded to; for a much larger proportion of the aborigines goes to Christianity and Hinduism than to Islam.

The particulars now mentioned, eight in number, all bear directly on the question of the numerical progress of Islam. We are persuaded that, taking India as a whole, it is not gaining on Hinduism. There is, however, one small district in which it has been making progress for many years past—that of British Malabar, on the west coast of Southern India, in which we find that fiercely fanatical sect the Moplahs. Notably enough, in the neighbouring native states of Cochin and Travancore Islam does not advance. On the whole, the advance, even in British Malabar, does not count for much.

Whatever may be the case as to numbers, it is certain that, in position and influence throughout India, Islam has long been declining. Old families are decaying, and few new ones are taking their place. Hitherto the Moslem has looked scowlingly on that Western education, of which the more pliant Hindu has eagerly availed himself; and thus the Mohammadans are gradually elbowed out of Government appointments. Earnest efforts have been made by the authorities to make them fit themselves for the public service, and once and again hopes have been expressed that a "new era" was commencing. At Alighar, in Bengal, also, a vigorous attempt has been made by the enlightened Sir Syed Ahmed to give a really good education to his co-religionists. It is interesting. Will it be successful? Not improbably. Further, in so far as true knowledge spreads among Mohammadans, it may help them to retain their position, but it will still more certainly impair their bigotry—their boundless scorn and hatred of all religions save their own.

There seems to be a general impression that the number of converts to Christianity from Islam is far smaller than from Hinduism; but in proportion to the amount of work done for them, conversions from the one faith have been as numerous as from the other. Missionaries who labour among Indian Musulmans have no cause for discouragement. True, the Moslems have not flocked, like the Hindus, to Christian schools. Mahomet has not come to the missionary; and the missionary, having his hands full of other work, has too seldom gone to Mahomet. Still there have been not a few most satisfactory cases of conversion from among Mohammadans in India.

In India Islam has greatly mixed with Hinduism. But when education spreads among Indian Musulmans—as sooner or later it is sure to do—great religious changes are inevitable. Even already a liberal and lax Islam has begun to appear. It manifests, and will increasingly manifest, a tendency to resolve itself into simple theism. This implies a new attitude, not only towards Mohammadan traditions, most of which are exceedingly foolish, but towards the Koran itself. A greatly reformed Islam, with its chief seat in India, may very possibly become a powerful factor in the religious history of the world. But this will be Mohammadanism in little more than name.

These, then, are our conclusions—at least not rashly come to—on the much-debated question of the state of Islam in India.

> "Si quid novisti rectius istis,
> Candidus imperti ; si non, his utere mecum."

Indian Archipelago.—The islands that lie between the Asiatic continent and Australia are often called Netherlands-India ; and we cannot but suspect that the belief that Islam is advancing in Hindustan arises from a confounding of the two regions. The part of Eastern Asia that belongs to Holland contains, it is probable, nearly thirty millions of inhabitants. Almost nine-tenths of these are Mohammadans, at least in name. Islam is still gaining converts ; perhaps about 10,000 a year. Christianity annually receives half this number—about 5000—drawn from both Islam and heathenism. The converts from the former during the last twenty years in Java alone have been more than 10,000.[1] In the Moluccas the Gospel now spreads faster than Islam.

We are sorry to say that, as regards religion, the conduct of the Dutch authorities in the East has been most culpable in a Christian point of view, as well as politically disastrous. They have smiled on Mohammadanism; they have frowned on Christian missions.[2] Now, however, they have taken alarm; for Islam of late, glorying in its strength, has manifested a bitter hatred of all that is Christian or European, and Holland has begun to tremble for her Eastern empire. Let us hope that she will not now rush to the opposite extreme, and,—as formerly in Ceylon,—blight with excessive patronage the true spirit of Christian missions.

The Negro Races.—We come now to speak of Mohammadanism among the Negro races of Africa. On this subject there has been of late much vehement discussion, chiefly since Canon Isaac Taylor read a paper on the subject. The views expressed by him have attracted notice mainly because they are those of a clergyman of the Anglican Church; in themselves, they indicate no exact knowledge

---

[1] We have obtained this information from Dr. Schreiber, secretary of the Rhenish Missionary Society, and from friends in Holland.

[2] "Dem Islam ist ausgedehnter Vorschub geleistet worden; während die Mission ängstlich verhindert und beschränkt wurde."—Dr. Gundert (*Die Evangelische Mission*, s. 218).

of facts, and little power of reasoning. A writer from whom he largely borrows has earnestly repudiated his "crudities," and censured his "headlong heedlessness."[1] We may, therefore, leave the Canon alone.

Livingstone declared that he had seen no missionary zeal among Mohammadans in Africa. Mohammadan slave-drivers in abundance; "the land like the garden of Eden before them, and behind them a desolate wilderness;" and the cruelties which he had witnessed, he tells us, haunted his dreams and made him start up from sleep in horror. He further reminds us that the Koran has not been translated into any African tongue. The slaves are circumcised, but neither instructed nor released from slavery—Moslem thus tyrannising over Moslem. Arabs speak of Negroes as *gumu* or callous. So far the great missionary. But while all this is true

---

[1] Mr. Bosworth Smith. See *Nineteenth Century,* December 1887. He writes still more indignantly about the Canon's "invincible ignorance" in the *Times* of December 29. We differ from Mr. B. Smith's estimate of Mohammad, and hold with such scholars as Sprenger and Muir. But the paper now referred to is able and comprehensive, and has many just views powerfully expressed. It is to be regretted that the writer of it has never seen Mohammadanism *in situ.*

Mr. B. Smith and some other writers speak of Islam and Christianity as "kindred" religions. Kindred in what sense? "A little more than kin and less than kind." Not kindred in spirit. Nay, Islam overturns the very foundation of distinctive Christianity by denying the crucifixion of the Son of God.

of Southern and South-Eastern Africa, it does not fully apply to Central and Western Africa, north of the equator. Mohammadan influence has been extending for the last twelve hundred years over the Soudan, and to within six, or perhaps four, degrees of the line.

And how extending? Pre-eminently through war and conquest. We must not forget the words of Hallam: "The people of Arabia, a race of strong passions and sanguinary temper, inured to habits of pillage and murder, found in the law of their native prophet not only a license, but a command to desolate the world."[1] War for the extension of Islam was solemnly commanded in the name of Heaven; and in twenty-seven military expeditions Mohammad himself set the horrible example, which throughout all succeeding generations his followers have only too closely copied.

The unhappy Negroes have been an easy prey. They are slaughtered like sheep; for in most cases their discipline is poor and their arms are few. The Arabs, on the contrary, are not only, as Burckhardt says, "a nation of robbers," but a nation of born soldiers.

But there are Moslem missionaries, we are told, who are contented with simple preaching. We wait for evidence as to their success, and as to the

[1] History of the Middle Ages, chap. vi.

means they use; since forcible conversion, wherever needed, is binding on the missionary. Meantime, we shudder at the accounts given by such men as Lander and Schweinfurth as to the character of the Moslem missionaries. If these experienced travellers are not entirely wrong, the so-called missionaries are often the vilest of the vile.

And what do they teach? They teach the Negroes to repeat in Arabic the words, "There is no God but Allah, and Mohammad is Allah's messenger." The Koran is to the Negro—often to his Arab teacher—a book of incantations and spells. Written texts are worn as amulets; or the writing is washed off and drunk. Alas for the "exalted ideas of the Divinity" which, we are told, Islam communicates to the Negro fetish-worshipper! He mostly retains his old ideas.[1] Even if he imbibed the Koranic idea, what would it be? Was the traveller Palgrave wrong when he called it "monstrous and blasphemous"?[2] Was he wrong when he said

---

[1] But what are these? Is Dr. Blyden right? He says: "On the continent of Africa, in spite of the fetishes and greegrees which many of them are supposed to worship, there is not a single tribe which does not stretch out its hands to the great Creator" (Christianity, Islam, and the Negro Race, p. 132). How far, then, does Islam raise them to higher conceptions?—Further, some have talked as if there were no civilised Negro states,—as if civilisation came only with the Arabs. This is a great mistake.

[2] See "Travels through Central and Western Arabia," by W. G. Palgrave.

that Allah has "one main feeling" towards His creatures, viz., "jealousy," lest they "encroach" on His kingdom and claims? The language is strong, and we will not fully commit ourselves to it; but the fact that so well-informed a traveller can use it may give some writers pause.

Slavery, polygamy, divorce at pleasure, intolerance in religion—these are not excrescences, but of the essence, of Islam. To convert men to such a faith is easy. If Islam stops intoxication among its converts, good; but does it? Unhappily no; or to a very small extent. At best, the acceptance of Islam will raise men to the Arab civilisation of the seventh century; but it will fix them there. Progress is then possible only by casting it away. The best thing that we can say about Negro converts to Islam is that they imbibe so little of it. "A little knowledge" may in this case not be "a dangerous thing,"—possibly advantageous; yet assuredly if they "drink deep," they will proportionally become fanatical and stern.

We do not for a moment admit that Islam is better fitted than the Gospel for the Negroes in their present state, though we have said that a lower religion will be more readily accepted than a higher. Nor need we at all despair of the advance of the Gospel among the Black races. Missionaries like Dr. Leighton Wilson, who spent many years in

West Africa, speak of them as "social, generous, confiding;" and affirm that the "beauty and consistency" of religion is exemplified by the Christian Negro better than any other. Mrs. Beecher Stowe did not draw wholly on imagination when she delineated the character of "Uncle Tom;" and Emin Pasha has lately said, "The Black race in valour and courage is inferior to no other; in devotion and self-denial, it is superior to many. . . . They are capable of progress."[1]

Nor can we hold that the Negro is even in point of intellect essentially inferior to many of the

[1] Of late, various writers—especially Mr. Froude—have taken a very discouraging view of the state and prospects of the Negro race. But we might quote a host of witnesses who speak in very different terms. Let the following suffice. Lord Brassey says that "the capabilities of the coloured races are nowhere seen to greater advantage than in Sierra Leone. They supply the official staff of the Government. A coloured barrister of marked ability is the leader of the Bar, and makes a professional income of £3000 a year." (See *The Mail*, 16th December 1887.) The Bishop of Jamaica sends home a letter written by one of his clergy, in which the steady progress of the Negroes in Jamaica in honesty, truthfulness, and regard for marriage is strongly affirmed. Farther, "nothing is more striking than their temperance." During the celebration of the Queen's Jubilee in Kingston the only drunk persons seen by the writer were whites. (See *Guardian*, January 25, 1888.) With regard to the Negroes in the Southern States of America, "The Church at Home and Abroad" (Presbyterian) quotes approvingly the following words:—"The coloured people of the South are making wonderful advances in material prosperity. . . . The attainments in learning and eloquence of not a few of them have been noticed with surprise."

proudest races. Toussaint L'Ouverture, Frederick Douglas (half Negro), Bishop Crowther, Dr. Blyden, —these names at once occur to us, and others could easily be added, as proving that Negro capacity is often high. But the Negro has never had fair play; nor has he yet. We boast of having given him emancipation; but you may strike the fetters off his body, and yet make the iron enter his soul, perhaps only the deeper. The haughty Aryan race condescends to welcome Shemitic and Mongolian converts; but, in its daintiness, it barely tolerates the Negro. What is our religion worth if this feeling is to last? Let us leave all pride of race to the Brahman. Let us remember that the believing Negro is a child of God as much as any of us—dearer, it may be, because of his simple faith, to the heart of the Father, than we with all our boasted superiority of intellect and civilisation. Let us respect the Negro, and so teach him to respect himself.

But observe how our missions are weighted by this wicked scorn of the Blacks. The Arabs hardly have the feeling. From before the days of Mohammad the Arab and Negro have freely intermingled, and not unfrequently intermarried. The dark skin is no bar to advancement. Men distinguished in Mohammadan history have been Negroes. The Arab accepts the Negro convert as a brother. Our missions will have fair play when we shall do the same. Meantime we heartily rejoice that a due position has been given by the Church Missionary Society to such men as Bishop Crowther and Archdeacon Johnson, and to Bishop Holly of Haiti and Bishop Fergusson of Liberia by the Protestant Episcopal Church of America; and that non-Episcopal societies have not a few ordained Negro preachers.

We must still refer to one appalling evil—the traffic in intoxicating drink, so eagerly pushed by many traders in Africa. Portugal, Britain, France, the United States—are all offenders in this matter, and far above the rest, Germany.[1] That professedly Christian nations should carry on this hideous traffic is deplorable; and if really Christian men have any share in it, it is high time that they should realise the horrible consequences of what they do. Most touching was the appeal made a short time ago to Bishop Crowther by the Mohammadan chief Malike, entreating him to put a stop to what was ruining his people. Drink seems almost as withering a curse

[1] The Rev. Horace Waller, an old companion of Livingstone's, has published a striking pamphlet, entitled "Trafficking in Liquor with the Natives of Africa." His tables show that Britain exports to Africa twice as much liquor as America, and Germany (chiefly from Hamburg and Bremen) nearly seven times as much as Britain. This, then, is as foul a blot on German character as the opium traffic is on that of the British Government in India.

to miserable Africa as the slave-trade itself. Unless the plague can be stayed, the inevitable issue is the extermination of all whom it reaches.

It is some consolation to think that all traders in Africa are not involved in this condemnation. Thus the "African Lakes Company" has operations extending from Quillimane to Lake Tanganyika, but traffic in intoxicating drink it utterly abjures. And there are other companies, and doubtless individual traders, that are equally free of the leprosy.

IV.

MODES OF MISSIONARY ACTION.

Let us first inquire what these are, and then whether they require to be modified in order that greater results may follow.

"The great work of evangelising the heathen ought not to be restricted to any one method. Every mode of operation that manifests the spirit of the Gospel, every civilising influence that the missionary can bring to bear on the people, and that gives to Christianity a practical aspect, lies within the scope of the Divine commission."[1] The general truth of these weighty words will hardly be disputed.

The great modes of missionary activity have been the following:—The preaching of the Word; the education of the young; and the circulation of the Holy Scriptures and religious books. Various missions, especially German ones, have had industrial operations; but these have not been so

[1] Mr. John Lowe in his work on Medical Missions.

common among civilised races. In recent days, Medical Missions have assumed much prominence. They have been especially favoured by Britain and America; but Germany, too, is beginning to employ them, especially the Basle, Bremen, and Moravian Missions.

There is another mode of extending the Gospel which we may call unofficial,—we mean the influence exerted by converts on their countrymen in social intercourse.

Now it is a most interesting question, Can we estimate the amount of blessing which has rested on these modes of activity respectively?

An experienced Chinese missionary, Dr. Nevius, has mentioned his impressions on this subject. Beginning with the kind of work which seems to have had least effect, he states the order thus:—

1. Bible-distribution,
2. Tract-distribution,
3. Preaching in chapels,
4. Translation and literary work,
5. Schools,
6. Preaching on missionary tours,
7. Private social intercourse.

Dr. Nevius holds the last-mentioned mode to have been exceedingly influential. In fact, he reckons that "by far the greater number of baptisms" is to be referred to the influence of private social intercourse. We understand him to mean social intercourse between Christian and heathen natives. The Rev. D. MacIvor also affirms that "seven-eighths" of the conversions that have occurred in his mission have been traceable to the influence of Native Christians—not recognised officially as evangelists—on their heathen friends and neighbours. This is important testimony.

The statement of Dr. Nevius does not include Medical Missions or women's work among women. The value of these stands relatively high in the list.

Dr. Nevius has made a valuable estimate; but it would be rash to say it holds universally. Moreover, we must remember that, in almost every case of conversion, there has been a concurrence of influences, and that it can hardly be traced to any single cause.

Bible Distribution.

It is probable that many will be surprised at the comparatively little effect assigned to the circulation of the Holy Scriptures. But we must remember that, to an uninstructed heathen, many parts of the Bible are difficult of comprehension. When it is circulated among professing Christians—say, of the Eastern Churches—the result is usually much more striking. Among Mohammadans, too, Bible-distribution is fitted to do much good; for the Moslem have already a considerable knowledge of Scriptural names and facts.

Preaching.

We need hardly say a word on the importance of the third and sixth modes of usefulness—preaching—whether carried on in chapels or in the open air, whether as repeated in the same locality, or on extended missionary tours. Each plan is useful in its own way. If possible, places already visited should be revisited several times.

We presume missionaries are generally agreed that, in preaching, attacks on heathenism should seldom be made. It generally irritates; it drives off rather than draws. Brahmans, and still more so Musulmans, are often anxious for discussion, and it is not always possible to avoid it; but the missionary will extricate himself from its entanglements as speedily as possible and lovingly proclaim the glad tidings of salvation. Kind entreaty will seldom or never fail to soften and impress. Hard, unfeeling argument will do no good; in fact, it will do harm.

While we say this, we hold that missionaries should have mastered the systems of faith with which they deal, and be ready, on fitting occasions, to show that they have done so. Otherwise their shunning of controversy will be misunderstood.

It is a great matter when a missionary can not only preach, but sing. A sweet, tender hymn reaches farther than a strong argument. " A verse may find him who a sermon flies," as George Herbert well says.

In recent discussions on the relative progress of Christianity and Islam in Africa, it has several times been asserted that, in preaching to the heathen, missionaries inculcate " unthinkable and transcendental dogmas." Such is not our experience. The preaching we have heard has dwelt especially on the life and death, the miracles and parables, of the Lord Jesus Christ. Each fact, miracle, or parable forms a picture which the rudest Pagan mind can easily perceive. It is not the doctrines of the Gospel that repel the heathen. It is the life it prescribes. Among Hindus, at all events, if a missionary would lower the Bible-standard, he might soon have a threefold or tenfold number of converts.

Translation and Literary Work.

Translations of valuable works into the languages of India, as well as the composition of original productions, must be regarded as of the greatest possible importance. Such books are required both for the growing Christian population and the non-Christian communities. A pure literature—there is not at this moment a more pressing want in India, China, and Japan. The Christian Vernacular Education Society, which was formed in the year of the Mutiny, under the presidency of Lord Shaftesbury,[1] has done excellent work for India; but its revenue is far too small. A similar society has recently been formed for China, which, we trust, may effect much good. Happily, in India at least, native authorship of a high class is by no means scanty. Already even Hindu ladies are doing valuable service with their pens. The late Toru Dutt of Calcutta, for example, who was a truly remarkable proof of the grace and refinement which the Hindu woman can attain under the elevating influence of the Gospel, wrote English in prose and verse with singular correctness and taste.

Schools.

There was at one time in influential quarters a prejudice against schools as an evangelistic agency; but it seems largely to have passed away.

We know of no work more precious, more delicate, and more difficult than that of teaching the Gospel to heathen children. To do it rightly will require the best energies of the best men in every mission.

---

[1] Now under that of Lord Northbrook.

Education of a higher kind has been carried farthest in India and among the Christian communities of the East. In India the powerful advocacy of Dr. Duff gave it great prominence; and the Scottish Churches have had in India much the largest share of the higher education. For a long time mission institutions were put to a great disadvantage by the exclusive patronage which Government gave its own purely secular colleges; but more justice has of late been done to both missionary and native institutions. In accordance with the great Despatch on education of 1854, Government ought to withdraw gradually from direct connection with all the higher education. Not only is it pledged to do so, its colleges are far more expensive than others. Moreover, it does not, and cannot, rightly educate; for what is the value of instruction purely secular? Even the natives have often deplored the absence of moral and religious teaching in Government institutions. Some time ago the First Prince of Travancore quoted with high approbation the assertion of Pestalozzi that intellectual teaching by itself is positively "pernicious." To toss the mind of India out of superstition into unbelief is strange work on the part of a Christian Government, and the results must be deplorable. Can men sow the wind and *not* reap the whirlwind? Therefore let Government hand over to other bodies, native or missionary, the task it cannot of itself perform. Quite enough, and more than enough, remains for it in the elementary teaching of the masses (which Government has far too much neglected, and in which the infidelising process hardly comes into play), and in the maintenance of colleges for law, medicine, engineering, and technology generally.[1]

ALL CHRISTIAN COLLEGES OUGHT TO BE ENDOWED. It is interesting to note that America, which does not believe in endowing churches, sedulously and munificently seeks to endow its colleges, whether at home or abroad. When will Britain follow the example, and put its missionary colleges on a strong and stable basis?

With regard to popular education in India, it is desirable that the missions should have many of their converts trained as teachers. Not a few of

---

[1] Since these words were written, the Government of India has addressed a long despatch to the Local Governments on the subject of discipline and moral training in schools. It begins by admitting that the extension of education has in some measure resulted in the "growth of tendencies unfavourable to discipline and favourable to irreverence." Governments are slow to admit mistakes. Let the Indian Government receive the meed of praise due to a candid confession which means so much. Unhappily, the remedies it suggests will be of little avail.

A native gentleman of high position—the present Sheriff of Madras—lately expressed himself thus on a great public occasion:—"The country needs a radical change in the character of its training schools.... The elaboration of a system of Technical Education has become a great necessity."

these might set up schools of their own, receiving grants-in-aid from Government. The occupation would be sufficiently remunerative. In all such schools the great truths of natural religion could be inculcated, without giving the slightest offence to Hindus or Mohammadans, and probably with their decided approbation. We believe that, in many cases, the Christian Scriptures could be read and explained, as is done in Travancore.[1]

We have been speaking of education as an evangelistic agency. It is unnecessary to dwell on the necessity of thorough Christian training for the children of converts. Nothing can exceed this in importance. Already, in consequence of their Christian education, the children of converts are steadily rising in the scale of society.

MEDICAL MISSIONS.

Of the vast importance of Medical Missions in every part of the foreign field, it seems hardly necessary to say a word. In Mohammadan lands like Turkey and Persia, in which direct preaching of the Gospel

[1] In the school at Trivandrum, under the direct patronage of the Hindu Government of Travancore, the Christian Scriptures are regularly studied. We found there a Syrian Christian diligently teaching the Gospel of St. Matthew to Hindus, several of whom were Brahmans. Apparently they were much interested in the lesson.

is compassed with so much difficulty, a medical missionary would have abundant opportunities of doing good. The office of the physician is held in the highest esteem by all Mohammadans; and no man could enjoy more direct access to the hearts of the Moslem than a Christian physician bent on doing good to both soul and body. Even when he could not preach, his life would be a sermon.

Specially valuable are Female Medical Missions, since, as a rule, the women of the East are accessible only to women. Would that for every lady-doctor now in India and China we had a thousand! It is deplorable to think that, for generations to come, there will be an immensity of physical suffering, especially among women and children, which medical skill could remove,—aye, and of premature death, which could easily be prevented.[1]

On the whole, in reference to the various modes of evangelistic effort, we have little or no change to propose. Each form of effort has been blessed, and doubtless, in the goodness of God, will continue to

[1] We heartily rejoice in the effort made, under the presidency of the Countess of Dufferin, to meet this great evil. Lady Dufferin wrote on 25th October 1887 that the Jubilee Fund for this object amounted to five lakhs of rupees—say nearly £40,000. By 31st December the sum of 9331 rupees seems to have been added. May all success attend the scheme! Yet we must remember that the Zenana Medical Missions have a still higher aim, since they minister to the soul as well as to the body.

be so. We still call attention to the most powerful of all agencies—that of private, unofficial effort on the part of native Christians. " Every man a missionary,"—every man a mirror, receiving and reflecting light;—let that be more and more the cry of the rising Churches in Heathendom. Yet we do not require to press this as an exhortation; for it *is* their cry more and more, and therefore do we feel assured that the final triumph is hastening on.

There is another form of effort that is fitted to do much good—we mean visits of earnest Christian men from Europe. Addresses to natives may in India be given in many cases in English, and in other cases through interpreters. This kind of work is not new; but it is increasing. Thus, a Winter Mission, consisting of six clergymen and two laymen, has this season been sent out by the C. M. S. for work among Christians and heathens in India. It has been warmly welcomed, and seems to be doing much good. Such deputations should not be limited to India.

But when the truth has been published and men have separated from heathenism, what follows? The converts have to be gathered into congregations for public worship, the preaching of the Word, and the administration of the sacraments. For such purposes Paul and Barnabas "ordained elders in every church." We presume it will be universally admitted that their example should be followed as soon as suitable office-bearers can be found. For the office of pastor native converts should be carefully trained.

But congregations should not remain isolated. How should they be associated? Here we come on the question of Church-government; which we will not polemically discuss. Three great forms of it exist—the Congregationalist, Presbyterian, and Episcopalian.

In Christendom even Congregationalists have their denominational "Unions." In Heathendom such unions are absolutely necessary, as a minimum.

Presbyterian missions will naturally unite the native congregations under Presbyteries, Synods, and General Assemblies. Episcopalians will appoint Bishops with dioceses.

But everything must be done with a view to render the Mission Churches as soon as possible independent of foreign control. They will of themselves demand this; but it is, at any rate, necessary to their healthy growth and extension. Self-support must go along with self-government; it

MODES OF MISSIONARY ACTION.

will seldom precede. Of course, when foreign support and control have ceased, there should still remain loving and frequent intercourse between the Mother Churches and their daughters in Heathendom.

V

WHAT NEXT?

1. ENLARGEMENT of effort, far more than change of methods, is required; but how vast is the necessary enlargement!

Here the tone of joy in which we have been speaking must be laid aside. Undoubtedly our first duty is sorrowful confession of neglect and earnest pleading for forgiveness, with a determination, God helping us, to bring forth fruits meet for repentance.

What Christian can rest satisfied with the pittance now raised for the conversion of the heathen?[1] It is little more than two millions for all Protestant missions. Lack of funds indicates lack of feeling. Contrast this with the enormous sums spent on amusements, or on intoxicating drink (about 130 millions), or on tobacco, in the United Kingdom alone. When the contrast is first mentioned to any

[1] In the Churches of North America it is said to be $\frac{1}{105}$th part of 1 per cent. of income.

Christian assembly, the hearers can hardly believe the figures to be correct.

Again, are we satisfied with the proportion of labourers going forth to reap the fields that are white unto the harvest? In round numbers, we have sent forth 3000 ordained ministers, 730 laymen, and 2500 women—chiefly the wives of missionaries. Three thousand missionaries for all Heathendom! Why, the Presbyterian portion of Scotland has a larger number. If Scotland, with all the auxiliary influences of family instruction, schools, city missionaries, &c., &c., requires a minister for every thousand inhabitants, then how many does Heathendom require? But even give the same proportion, and we need, for every one man already sent, to provide about three hundred. We by no means forget that one of our chief endeavours must be to raise up native labourers, preachers, and teachers. Still, the foreign staff requires much enlargement even in countries like India and China; and we are reminded of Xavier's passionate outcry: "It often comes into my mind to go round all the Universities of Europe, crying like a madman to all the learned men there, whose learning is greater than their charity, 'Ah! what a multitude of souls is, through your fault, shut out of heaven!'" And to those who reply that, in these enlightened days, few believe in that melancholy consequence, we say, as Mr. Spurgeon said some time ago, "The question is not whether the heathen will be saved if they do not hear the Gospel, but whether you will be saved if you do not send them the Gospel." The command is peremptory; the duty is prompt obedience.[1]

2. Lack of interest in missions largely depends on lack of knowledge. How shall the knowledge be enlarged?

We must by no means overlook the immense importance of the pulpit in this connection. If no missionary fire burn in the pulpit, the pews will be icy cold. We trust that more and more systematically the great subject is presented to their flocks by ministers of religion. Striking facts can be drawn from mission history with which the preacher can illustrate and enforce his teaching. And ought a single Lord's day to pass in which there is not in the prayers pointed allusion to the work among both Jews and Gentiles? Whatever difficulty there may be in regard to this in congregations which worship in fixed liturgical forms, there is no difficulty when extempore prayer is offered.

Certainly we do not overlook the value of addresses

---

[1] As to the wants of Indian women alone, in 1880 Sir Salar Jung wrote that no fewer than 1025 medical women, educated in England, were absolutely necessary for India *as a beginning;* but that even that number was "wholly insufficient." On the British register there were in 1887 only 54!—*Dr. Jex Blake.*

delivered by missionaries who are fresh from the field abroad; we do not overlook the value of the great "May Meetings," and similar reunions; we do not overlook the value of books on missions; but still the great propelling power must be put forth in the ordinary ministrations of the multitudinous pulpits of Europe and America. At the same time, we cannot dispense with any auxiliary influences. In Sunday-schools, in addresses to children, and family teaching, what subject could be more attractive to the young? With all earnestness we would insist on the importance of parental influence in this connection. The future Brainerd or Martyn may best receive the first impulse to a missionary life at his mother's knee; and surely many a Christian mother would feel it a high privilege to instil the feeling of self-sacrifice into a son or daughter's soul. There is reason to fear that hitherto, even in pious households, the influence of parents, brothers, sisters, has been to discourage, rather than encourage, those members of the family who sought to dedicate themselves to the missionary life; but when the zeal for missions rises, as ere long it will rise, to the height of a holy passion, all this will change, and every Christian family will rank it among its selectest honours that one of its number has gone forth to the high places of the field. We have all heard with admiration of the Spartan mother, so moved by devotion to her country that, as she sent forth her son to the battlefield, she presented him with a shield, and said, " *With* this, my son, or *on* it,"—that is, " Return in triumph with it, or be borne upon it dead; but fling it not, to save thy life, ingloriously away!" Cannot devotion to Christ raise a mother's heart as high as devotion to country ever did?

Let there be a holy rivalry among the Churches in this matter. For pious men to wage among each other vehement and even bitter controversy on points of no fundamental importance, while a thousand millions of the human race are perishing before their eyes, reminds us of John Foster's terrible comparison of the state of Christendom to a great battle raging in the antediluvian world, and hostile squadrons doing desperate deeds of valour against each other, while the universal deluge was rising round them.

3. We have spoken with much sorrow of the paltry sum which is as yet raised for missions. But we must not forget that already there are many zealous labourers in the field who receive no salary; they have gone forth at their own expense. All the ordained agents of the English " Universities' Mission " do so. The number of these volunteers, if we may call them so—but they may well belong to the regular army—ought very largely to increase.

We cannot rest content until multitudes whom God has blessed with a competence shall feel it their greatest honour to dedicate themselves and their possessions to the work abroad. We need men like Lord Shaftesbury in Heathendom as much as in Christendom. The noblest of the land ought to deem themselves still more ennobled by going "far hence unto the Gentiles." Does the assertion raise a smile? Why should it? We advocate no new thing. Columba and several of the old Celtic missionaries were of noble, or even princely, lineage. Has the Gospel lost the power it possessed a thousand years ago to move the higher as well as the lower classes? At a later time that truly remarkable missionary Raymond Lull was a nobleman of Majorca; or, coming to still later days, Xavier was a Portuguese of position. Scotland is still mourning over the early death of an Earl's son, the Hon. Ion Keith-Falconer, son of the Earl of Kintore, who had consecrated himself, with rich acquisitions in Oriental lore, to work among the Mohammadans of Arabia. He is dead, but his high example lives, and will not die.[1]

[1] Equally striking is the case of the Hon. J. H. H. Gordon, a son of the fifth Earl of Aberdeen. He was brought under deep religious impressions at the age of eighteen, and thenceforward was diligent in seeking to bring men to Christ. At the University of St. Andrews he was, according to Principal Shairp, "the favourite and flower of all his generation." So at Cambridge. A man of

And there are things in history more remarkable still. Nothing in the early annals of Buddhism is more striking than its missionary zeal. The praises which some are fain to lavish on it as a system of belief are sufficiently foolish; but we cannot note the efforts of its early professors to extend their religion without being lost in wonder. Their message was a message of despair; they could only assert that existence is misery, and the sooner it ceases the better. Yet they deemed the message true; they thought it might be of use to sorrow-stricken humanity, and therefore they hastened to publish it abroad; and, in doing so, they shunned not trackless deserts nor inhospitable mountains nor tempestuous oceans. Conspicuous among those extraordinary missionaries were the son and daughter of Asoka, the first Buddhist sovereign of India. The Prince Mahendo and the Princess Sanghamittā laid aside the purple robe of royalty, put on the yellow garments of the mendicant ascetic, devoted themselves to a missionary life, proceeded to the island of Ceylon—then tenanted by worshippers of

varied accomplishments; his religion bright and sunny. From an early period he had a desire to become a missionary. He intended to proceed to the Transkei Territory in British Kaffraria, and there, having purchased land, to carry on mission-work, assisted by a staff of Christian agents. He died in 1868. The "Gordon Memorial Mission" was founded by his relatives in connection with the death of this remarkable young man.

demons—and there lived and probably died as teachers of the new religion. What a lesson! What a rebuke to slumbering Christendom! Surely the self-denial of those old Buddhist missionaries is infinitely pathetic. Can it fail to shame us? Will it fail to rouse us?

4. We next speak of union and co-operation in Missions. It is a grand and extensive theme; but we can touch only on certain aspects of it.

We cannot possibly forget how our Blessed Lord, in His great intercessory prayer, pleads for the unity of His people, and with that unity connects the belief of the world in His Divine mission. It is a solemn question, What is the nature and extent of that unity? How far does it imply a visible, external, formal oneness; or how far would unity of heart and aim answer the great idea?

At all events, it is plain that we are far off from the state of which the Lord Jesus speaks. For example, there are now more than thirty-five Church organisations in India. We may be thankful that there has, on the whole, been not much of mutual collision, though collision there has been; but who can tolerate the idea of our European and American divisions being transplanted to the East and there perpetuated? Sectarian jealousies are deplorable at home; they would be ruinous abroad.

F

The missionaries see the necessity of union and are striving for its attainment. To a certain extent they are successful. In Japan, five Presbyterian bodies have coalesced into one Church; and the converts of three Episcopalian missions—two from England, the other from America, have done the same thing. So at Amoy in China, the English and American Presbyterians are blended in one Mission Church; and indeed they were the first to set the good example of such union. So, doubtless, other denominations will gravitate towards each other and gradually coalesce, until in each mission sphere there will be but one Episcopalian body, one Presbyterian, one Methodist, and so on. So far well.

But are these great divisions to be perpetuated in the mission-field? The question is deeply important, and demands earnest consideration.

We are disposed to think it will be solved chiefly by the Mission Churches themselves.[1] They will choose their own ecclesiastical polity. It will probably be no mere reproduction of any form, whether European or American. They say they will attempt to find, and possibly they may succeed in finding, a system which shall combine the merits

---

[1] Thus the Japanese Christians connected with the Episcopal Churches "avow their desire for an independent national Episcopal Church, separated for a time from the other Churches, but looking forward to union hereafter."—*C. M. S. Report*, 1886-87.

of each of the leading forms of Church order now existing in Christendom. Already in Japan an earnest effort is made to blend the leading characteristics of Presbytery and Congregationalism; and there are thoughts of a union more comprehensive still.

We do not say that there will be only one Church in each great mission-field. India consists of various nations, speaking various languages. Each great province may prefer to have its own Church; each Church may have its distinctive characteristics. But among these Churches there will be, we fervently trust, full intercommunion. No unchurching of each other. If not one Church in the strict sense, yet a grand confederation of Churches. If not incorporation, yet hearty co-operation. And in so far as this great ideal may be realised, the union of the Churches in Heathendom will react powerfully on our miserably divided Christendom. The teachers will perforce learn from the pupils.[1]

---

[1] The unity of spirit that exists among the Native Christians of India is truly beautiful. They freely intermingle, not understanding, and with difficulty tolerating, the ecclesiastical barriers which in Europe and America separate Christians from Christians. I was much struck with this unity in Calcutta on a remarkable occasion when the Brahmos appeared as three separate and irreconcilable bodies, while the Christians marched as one great company of brethren. This unity, thank God, remains unbroken. But the oneness and mutual love of Christians is exhibited on a far grander scale than this. The massacres at U-Ganda stirred the hearts of

Already there have been very important conferences of missionaries in the foreign field. There have been several provincial conferences in India, and there have been two great general ones, attended by missionaries gathered from all parts of the country, and, we may say, representing all the forms of Evangelic Protestantism. Great good has resulted from these "holy convocations." Important questions have been discussed, important information has been given; and the hearts of men have been more closely drawn together.

Missionary conferences at home are equally important. In particular, an interesting and useful one was held in London ten years ago; and one which, in several respects, was perhaps more important still, was previously held in Liverpool. Probably such conferences will henceforth be required once every five years.

converts in all parts of the world. Most touching letters of sympathy poured in on the C. M. S. Committee, not only from members of Anglican missions, but from others, *e.g.*, from Christians in Madagascar connected with the London Missionary Society, and from the pupils of the English Presbyterian Mission at Swatow in China. Yes, well said Keble—

> "No distance breaks the tie of blood—
> Brothers are brothers evermore.
> . . . . . .
> So is it with true Christian hearts;
> Their mutual share in Jesus' blood
> An everlasting bond imparts
> Of holiest brotherhood."

It is very probable that all Protestant Churches and Missionary Societies will soon unite in setting apart the same time annually for prayer and supplication on behalf of missions, and that in all parts of the world the missionaries who have gone forth will—along with the flocks they have gathered out of heathenism—rejoicingly fall in with the arrangement. Indeed, this is already done to a large extent; and we may expect that, at the General Missionary Convocation next June, the arrangements for this great annual concert of prayer may be finally completed.

5. Some warm friends of Missions think the time has come when the unevangelised portion of the world should be mapped out and divided by common consent among the great missionary bodies.[1] The conception is a grand one, whatever practical difficulties may at present stand in the way of its fulfilment. One thing must not be overlooked. Many fields of labour which are said to be occupied are occupied but nominally; one single man is perhaps toiling among a million of heathen; and any real occupation would require a double, triple, or quadruple number of workmen. There is a fascination about fresh enterprises which may easily carry us

[1] Especially the late Isaac Taylor, and more recently Mr. Arthington of Leeds and the Rev. Dr. Pierson of America.

away, and make us leave fainting labourers to sink forgotten at their posts, while we are pressing on to the " regions beyond." Still, the conception of thus dividing Heathendom is noble and inspiring; and we must struggle towards its practical accomplishment. Let us begin by each missionary body proposing to itself a definite high aim which it will strive to attain during the next decennial or quinquennial period; and let there be full understanding among the Churches as to what each hopes to accomplish. There would then be a generous, holy rivalry among the various regiments of the one grand army; each would begin to realise the magnitude of the contest; each would enter into the joys and sorrows of multitudinous " brethren in arms;" each would be stimulated to " do exploits," as the prophet says, in the cause of God and man. At present each regiment thinks almost exclusively of itself. There is no general plan of campaign. Each regiment chooses its own ground and fights its own battle. Hence narrow, sectional, almost selfish thoughts. What mere earthly campaign could be carried on in any such way to a successful issue?

VI.

CONCLUSION.

It is time that these remarks should draw to a close. To the best of our ability we have sought honestly to present the subject we have been discussing in both its aspects. We have compared the present with the past, and have spoken of the increase of evangelistic zeal, contrasting the something accomplished now with the nothing attempted before. We have also compared the work now done with the work that remains undone; and perhaps, as we have been doing so, a tone of sorrow, capable of being taken for a tone of despondency, may have been perceptible in the statement.

But in truth there is no cause for despondency. Sorrow is right, rebuke is right, but despondency is entirely wrong; for a new era in missions is beginning.

Nay, it has begun. More than ten years ago I was conversing on this subject with Dr. Duff. No man used stronger language than he in reference to the lack of missionary zeal among congregations at home. To him the heart of the Church seemed cold as ice, and he sorrowed over this with an exceeding sorrow. But when I ventured to say that there were indications in many quarters of awakening zeal, he said he too could see them, and that he believed a great change was coming on.

Since that time the spirit of Christians at home, like that of Paul at Athens, has been "stirred" within them, and is being stirred more and more. We have all been thinking more or less of the dishonour done to the True and Living God throughout Heathendom, and of the misery of those who dwell in the region of the shadow of death. The marvellous openings which, in nearly all lands, have been made for the proclamation of the Gospel have compelled attention; the large amount of blessing which God has made to rest on faithful work has in some degree warmed our hearts, and gratitude impels us to run the way of His commandments; and last, not least, a sense of our guilty neglect in the past now prompts the desire to make up for it, as far as in us lies, by double diligence in time to come. The Church, as if drugged with opiates, has slept a death-like sleep; but at least she now begins to ask, Have I not slumbered too long?

Now, for the first time in history, we can have some adequate idea of the grandeur of the commission, "Teach *all nations*."[1] Now, too, for the first time in history, all nations have been made accessible. We are first overwhelmed by the magnitude of the allotted task, and then the believing soul strives, with the help of God, to rise to the high occasion.

Many things have concurred to produce this happy change; among others, Mr. Moody's visit to this country. Not that he spoke of Foreign Missions; during his first visit he appeared purposely to shun the subject; but he spoke of Christ's love and His claims, and of perfect consecration on the part of believers; and these things, when understood and felt, enkindle missionary zeal.

Proofs of the awakening meet us almost everywhere. It is as when the soft breath of spring passes over the world, and gladdens at once a thousand regions with life and fragrance and beauty. "The winter is past, the rain is over and gone, the flowers appear on the earth, the time of the singing of birds has come, and the voice of the turtle is heard in our land."

Women are coming forward in rapidly increasing numbers to enter at doors which were shut and fast-barred for ages, but are now flying open on every hand. We need as many women as men in the

---

[1] We think this sentiment was lately expressed by the Bishop of London.

mission-field; and ere long we shall doubtless have them.

What a remarkable movement has there been among students—as at Edinburgh, Dublin, Cambridge, and now most of all in America![1] In America it is almost startling in its magnitude, as when the prophet says, "Thy heart shall fear and be enlarged." We have been too much disposed to measure the Divine heart by the narrowness of our own. Let us henceforth "expect great things and attempt great things!"

In the autumn of 1886, two young men, graduates of Princeton College, New Jersey, after spending some time under Mr. Moody, set out on an important work. They were the sons of missionaries, and born in India. Their purpose was to visit the colleges, and invite students to declare themselves "willing and desirous, God permitting, to be foreign missionaries." They carried out their plan, and, by the latest accounts, no fewer than 2200 persons (including more than 300 females) have declared their readiness to go forth to the heathen field.[2] They belong to the various Evangelical denominations. Above 300 are in Canada,

[1] The rapid addition of a hundred labourers to the "China Inland Mission" is also very remarkable.

[2] See a paper by Dr. M'Cosh, late President of Princeton College; it is quoted in the *Foreign Missionary* for May 1887. See also *Bombay Guardian*, January 7, 1888.

the rest are in the United States. We know few movements in mission history at all comparable to this. Dr. M'Cosh rightly speaks of it as laying on the Churches "an awful responsibility."

Doubtless the whole number of those who have thus " willingly offered themselves " will not become missionaries. Some may draw back when the first gush of feeling passes away ; others will be found disqualified by feeble health. But, when all abatements are made, it is a truly remarkable phenomenon. What is the duty of the Church in connection with it ? Thanksgiving, sympathy, assistance,— fervent thanksgiving, hearty sympathy, prompt and large assistance.

Some of the students who have thus responded to the call of Christ may go forth at their own expense, but many will require pecuniary help. At present the income barely suffices to supply the necessities of men already in the field ; and the missionary revenue of the American Churches requires to be more than doubled by the time the missionary band is ready to go forth,—and that, we presume, will be from three to five years hence. Our expectation, like our prayer, is that He who has touched the hearts of these young disciples will touch the heart of the whole membership of the Churches ; and that, when such numbers feel it a duty and an honour to GO, corresponding numbers will feel it a duty and an honour to GIVE. There is no lack of means ; let there be no lack of heart ! It will be unspeakably deplorable if, at such a crisis, the Churches shall slumber on.[1]

Hitherto missionaries, and all faithful Christians who have realised the actual condition of the heathen, have felt as the devoted Judson felt when this groan ascended from his deepest soul—" Will the Christian world ever awake ? Will means ever be used adequate to the necessities of the heathen

---

[1] The *Missionary Herald* of June 1887 contains an extract from a letter to the Treasurer of the American Board from a gentleman and his wife, who wish their names to be withheld, but send 5000 dollars—say £1000—to the Treasurer, with the remark that their hearts are greatly moved to hear of so many young men and women offering themselves as missionaries. So will many hearts be moved.

> "They come, they come, these brave young hearts,
>   Aflame with earnest zeal ;
> They come with hopes as high as heaven,
>   With purpose firm as steel.
>
> They come by scores, these brave young hearts,
>   From homes all o'er the land ;
> They come anointed of the Lord,
>   And led by His right hand.
>
> They come, they come ! God bless them all,
>   And speed them on their way !
> May others come, till all the world
>   Shall own Messiah's sway !"

These lines—which we quote not as highly poetical, but as being full of heart—were found written on a slip of paper at a meeting of the Prudential Board, 19th April, at which sixteen persons were appointed to the foreign field.

world? O Lord, send help! Our waiting eyes are unto Thee!" Such cries have pierced the heavens.

Therefore the Churches will not slumber on. And surely the man must be blind who cannot discern the signs of the times, who does not see that great things are at hand. To the question, "What may happen?" the best rejoinder is, "What may *not* happen?" Let us lift up our heads in the hope that "redemption draweth nigh,"—yea, "the time of the restitution of all things."

Of a great change recorded in Scripture it is said that "the thing was done suddenly." So, in the providence of God, the end often comes unexpectedly, even when a silent preparation has been going on long before. The fruit has been hanging on the tree, and little change has been from day to day perceptible; the ingathering has seemed scarcely drawing nearer. But the splendour of summer passes into the mellow magnificence of autumn, and then is "the fulness of the times," the fitness of the time. A great wind shakes the tree, and suddenly the ripened fruit can be gathered all around.

Dr. Marshman of Serampore was accustomed to say that the difficulty was not with the hearts of the heathen; it was with the heart of the Church, —its coldness, its contractedness. But the heart of the Church is being warmed and enlarged; the

Lord in many ways is stirring it; and probably movements both among the Jews and in Heathendom are at hand which will fill the languid world with astonishment. Let the heavens rejoice and let the earth be glad; for those "scenes surpassing fable," on which the eye of the seers of Israel delighted from afar to gaze, may ere long be "scenes of accomplished bliss."

Therefore let every Christian be full of prayer and hope. Let him say, in those words of Milton which rise almost to the sublimity of Holy Writ:—

"Come forth out of Thy royal chambers, O Prince of all the kings of the earth! Put on the robes of Thine imperial majesty! Take up that unlimited sceptre which Thine Almighty Father hath bequeathed Thee! *For now the voice of Thy Bride doth call Thee, and all creatures sigh to be renewed.*"

APPENDIX.

A.

Rise of Missionary Zeal since the Reformation.

Sweden.

The first Protestant Mission was sent out by Gustavus Vasa, king of Sweden, in the year 1559. It was established in order to evangelise the inhabitants of Lapland. About the year 1600 five churches were built for the Lapps. Later on, a minister was appointed to accompany them in their wanderings.

Holland.

Early in the seventeenth century the Dutch wrested from the Portuguese many of their territories in the East; and the question of the conversion of the natives soon engaged attention. Not only were men's ideas widened, their hearts were enlarged. The Dutch East India Company, which dates from 1602, had the conversion of the heathen as one of its professed aims. Various treatises appeared, advocating the cause of missions. Professor Walæus of Leyden established in 1622 an institute for training missionaries. Some admirable missionaries were sent out, and excellent work was done. Ere long the movement became political rather than religious; and, as the mere name of Christian secured the favour of Government, profession largely took the place of true conversion. In this way the Hollanders too closely followed the policy of their rivals, the Portuguese.

England and Scotland.

The possession of foreign settlements had led England to think of the duty of evangelising their inhabitants. When Sir Humphrey Gilbert led an expedition to America in 1583, he expressly included mission-work among the objects in view; he spoke of the necessity of having compassion on poor infidels, "captived of the devil." In 1628 the charter granted to the Massachusetts Company affirmed the duty of winning the natives of America "to the knowledge of the true God and Saviour." The seal of the Company bore the figure of an Indian, with these words on a scroll issuing from his mouth, "Come over and help us." In 1644 a petition signed by seventy ministers of religion in England and Scotland was presented to the Long Parliament, praying that steps might be taken for the evangelisation of the heathen in America and the West India Islands; and in 1648 Parliament issued a circular to all the congregations calling for contributions towards that object. In 1631 the celebrated John Eliot left England, and in 1646 he began his great work among the American Indians. He was only the first of a noble succession of men—the remarkable family of the Mayhews among them—who consecrated their entire lives to work among the heathen.

During the seventeenth century several of the most

distinguished men in England manifested a deep interest in the cause of Missions.

The plan of Cromwell to form a great Protestant Propaganda, embracing the whole world, was a very noble conception; but the times were too stormy to allow it to be carried into execution.

Very touching was the language of Baxter. When at the Restoration nearly two thousand ministers were forbidden to preach, he wrote thus: "My soul is much afflicted with thoughts of the world, and more drawn out in desire of its conversion than heretofore. I was wont to look little farther than England in my prayers, . . . or if I prayed for the conversion of the Jews, that was almost all. But now . . . there is nothing that lieth so heavy on my heart as the thought of the miserable nations of the earth. Could we but go among Tartars, Turks, and Heathen, and speak their language, I should be little troubled for the silencing of 1800 ministers."

The Hon. Robert Boyle, one of the founders of the Royal Society, was also deeply concerned about the spread of the Gospel. He paid the expense of publishing Bishop Bedell's translation of the New Testament into Irish, of a Malay version of the Gospels and Acts, and of Pococke's Arabic translation of Grotius's treatise *De Veritate Religionis Christianæ*. He also founded the Boyle Lectures for the refutation of Judaism, Paganism, Mohammadanism, Atheism, and Deism.

In the eighteenth century Bishop Berkeley formed the project of a Christian College at Bermuda for the purpose of extending the Gospel among the American Indians. He proceeded to America in 1728 at great personal sacrifice, and waited three years in the vain hope that Government would fulfil its promise of support. The attempt was worthy of the high Christian character of this distinguished man.

A Society was formed in 1649, called "A Corporation for Promoting and Propagating the Gospel in New England."[1]

The Society for Promoting Christian Knowledge was formed in 1698; and in 1701 the Society for the Propagation of the Gospel in Foreign Parts.

Both of the two last Societies, however, attended to the spiritual wants of English colonists more than those of the heathen. The former indeed sustained the Lutheran missions in India throughout last century. The latter only began missions to the heathen in the present century.

The charter of the East India Company, as given in 1698 and renewed in 1702, required that at every station there should be a chaplain who should learn the language of the country and instruct in religion the native servants of the Company.

Germany.

But we must now go back and note the rise of the missionary spirit in Germany. It is interesting to observe that its origin is traceable to the celebrated Grotius, a

---

[1] This is not the same as the well-known "Society for the Propagation of the Gospel." After the American War of Independence, it transferred its operations to New Brunswick and Nova Scotia. It still exists. It employs clergymen and teachers. It has lands in the provinces now mentioned, and in England.

Dutchman, but for some time Ambassador of Sweden at Paris. Seven students from Lübeck there came under his influence, and were moved to devote themselves to a missionary life. The most noted of these was Peter Heyling, son of a goldsmith of Lübeck. He left Paris in 1632, and proceeded by way of Malta and Alexandria, reaching Abyssinia in the end of 1634 or beginning of 1635. He was an uncommon man both in attainments and devotedness. His translation of the New Testament into Amharic was a valuable work.

From about the year 1664 a most earnest attempt was made by an Austrian nobleman, Ernst Von Welz, to arouse the Churches of Germany to a sense of their obligation to diffuse the Gospel among heathen races. The result was small, although the pleading was most pathetic. Von Welz proved by noble self-denial that he spoke from deep and conscientious conviction. He abandoned his title of Baron, was ordained to the office of missionary, devoted his fortune to the work, and proceeded to labour in Dutch Guiana. Here the admirable man soon died, *apparently* having done all he did in vain. But his memory is precious, and his example is surely most arousing.

We may next refer to the evangelistic zeal of one of the greatest men of modern days, the philosopher Leibnitz. The Berlin Academy was founded in 1700. Leibnitz had sufficient influence to introduce as part of its basis the resolution that the Society should "occupy itself with the propagation of the true faith and Christian virtue." So far as the Academy was concerned, the scheme of the philosopher fell to the ground; but the great conception bore fruit in various ways.

Scandinavia.

The next name that demands attention is that of Thomas von Westen, born at Trondhjem (Drontheim), in Norway. He was a man of rare devotedness. In 1710 he became pastor of Vedö, near his native place, and preached the truth with all earnestness and much success. But his heart was especially drawn out in pity towards the numerous heathen nomads in the north of the country. A college for training missionaries to labour among them was established by Government in 1716. Westen was appointed director. He made three laborious missionary journeys in the far north. His literary and other labours were incessant, and his ardent zeal was communicated to a number of devoted disciples.[1]

We may be said to enter on a new epoch with the establishment of the Danish Mission to Tranquebar in Southern India. Denmark, indeed, was only too slow in taking up this work. She had been trading with Southern India and in possession of Tranquebar for nearly a century, but nothing had been done for the conversion of the natives. Dr. Lütkens, the chaplain of King Frederick IV., when residing at Berlin, had come under the influence of both Spener and Francke, two of the most honoured names in the records of German piety. At his suggestion two German candidates of theology were ordained and sent out to Tranquebar in the end of 1705. These were Ziegenbalg and Plütschau. The mission, indeed, was German rather

---

[1] Herzog, in Schaff's Encyclopedia. See also Dr. F. Stevenson's "Dawn of the Modern Mission" for a vivid sketch of Westen's character. This remarkable man is too little known about.

than Danish. It received pecuniary support from the Danish Government, but Danish theologians gave it little sympathy. The main stay of the enterprise was Francke, who resided at Halle. The interest taken in the mission in Britain was greatly deepened by a visit paid by the excellent Ziegenbalg to Europe, including England, in 1714.

A real Danish mission was begun when Hans Egede, a Norwegian, proceeded as a missionary to Greenland in 1721. Egede was a man of truly consecrated life. Marvellous was his patience in pressing on the cold hearts of his countrymen the claims of the heathen for thirteen years before he was sent out. Egede in broken health left Greenland in 1736; but the mission still went on.

The Moravians.

Before this, however, another community had entered on the field with a lofty consecration which has ever since been an example and a rebuke to the rest of Christendom. We speak of the Moravians or United Brethren, whose efforts have been all along, in the words of William Wilberforce, " supported by a courage which no dangers can intimidate, and a quiet constancy which no hardships can exhaust."

The moving spirit in connection with these missions was Count Zinzendorf. He had been brought into contact both with Francke and Ziegenbalg; and a visit to Copenhagen in 1731 greatly strengthened his desire for the conversion of the heathen. In 1732 the community at Herrnhut sent out two missionaries to the West Indies, and early in 1733 two others to Greenland; and ere long the intense ardour of Zinzendorf seemed transfused into the whole Church. In six years from the time the missionaries had sailed for Greenland, the conversion of Kajarnak—than which none is more celebrated in missionary annals—added fresh fuel to the flame; and the small and poor Moravian brotherhood became a city set upon a hill, conspicuous far and wide. We are not concerned with the question whether the modes of work adopted by them were in all respects the wisest possible; whether, for example, they did not too long overlook the importance of training a native ministry;[1] but in their ardent longing for the conversion of souls and the maintenance of a high standard of personal piety among the converts, they have all along been nobly eminent. About one in sixty of their adult members becomes a missionary to the heathen. The parent Church numbers only one-third of the converts gathered out of Heathendom.

England and Scotland.

Until near the end of the eighteenth century, the interest in missions, as exhibited in England, was lamentably small. The Society for the Propagation of the Gospel in Foreign Parts was languid. Somewhat less so was the Society for Promoting Christian Knowledge.

In 1709 a Society for Propagating Christian Knowledge was formed in Scotland, which, however, did no work among the heathen before 1740. Among the agents it then employed among the Indians was the truly admirable David Brainerd, whose journals and touching history, as described by Jonathan Edwards, have been blessed to multitudes. Towards the middle of the century Dod-

[1] See Warneck, p. 57.

dridge laboured at Northampton to kindle missionary zeal and send out labourers; but even his high character and earnestness could not arouse the heart of England from its deplorable apathy. Religion never was at a lower ebb in England. Utter unbelief prevailed in many quarters (as Butler testifies in his preface to the "Analogy"); and in others there was freezing indifference. But the miserable state of things had driven the few believing men to earnest and united prayer both in Britain and America. We may especially refer to the correspondence that took place between earnest Christian men in Scotland and New England, and to the arousing appeal of Jonathan Edwards, entitled "An humble attempt to promote explicit agreement and visible union among God's people in extraordinary prayer for the advancement of Christ's kingdom on earth." It appeared in 1746. Ere long Wesley and Whitfield were made the instruments of a glorious revival. That, of course, aroused an interest in missions; for warm evangelical life is necessarily evangelistic. In the providence of God, various causes combined to quicken the new current of thought. Among the chief of these were the great discoveries that had been made in distant regions by Captain Cook and others, and the new facilities of communication between one part of the world and another. Knowledge of the world became larger, clearer; and the condition of their fellow-creatures in lands hitherto unheard of could not fail to occupy the attention of Christian men.

This brings us down to Carey's time. See p. 6.

B.

INDIAN MISSIONARY STATISTICS.

The following figures, derived from the Decennial Statistical Tables, will give a fair view of the progress made by the Protestant Missions in India during ten years.

Description.	1871.	1881.
Stations	522	716
Foreign Agents, Ordained	548	658
Native ,, ,,	381	674
Congregations	2,972	4,538
Native Christians	318,363	528,590
Communicants	78,494	145,097
Male pupils	111,372	168,998
Female pupils	31,580	65,761
Sunday school pupils	...	83,321
Zenana houses visited	1,300	9,566

C.

BRITISH CONTRIBUTIONS TO FOREIGN MISSIONARY WORK.

The following statement is not very satisfactory; but, all the more on that account, it ought to be pondered:—

Canon Scott Robertson finds that, for the year 1886, the British Isles contributed less by £33,237 to foreign missionary work than they did for 1885. The total for 1886 was £1,195,714. Of this amount, £486,082 was contributed through Church of England societies; £193,617 through unsectarian or joint societies; £330,128 through Nonconformist societies; £177,184 through Scotch and Irish Presbyterian bodies; and £8,703 through Roman Catholic societies."

D

Present State of Educated Hindus.

For some time past there has been, in various parts of India, a somewhat remarkable state of mind among the educated. The Bombay *Subodh Patrika*, a high-class, well-informed paper, conducted on theistic principles, has lately expressed itself as follows (15th February 1888):—

"The religious condition of the generality of educated Hindus fills us with alarm. Faith in the old religion has disappeared. No one, we make bold to say, believes in the Vedas as inspired." The editor mentions a large number of prescribed rites which educated Hindus entirely neglect. He adds: "Drinking has made frightful progress."

He then proceeds to speak of a remarkable reactionary movement, which is comparatively new.

"Bad as the condition of the educated Hindu is, it is rendered far worse by the reaction that has come over us. The reactionists make the loudest professions of their faith in current Hinduism, the most essential precepts of which they violate in secret, and on all occasions they appear as the most vigorous champions of the religion."

This "studied insincerity" the *Subodh Patrika* condemns as "sapping the very foundations of morality." The editor is not a Christian; but all Christians will deeply sympathise with him in his lamentation over this deplorable state of things. The men he refers to are loudly calling for political reform, but never seem to think of moral reform in their own hearts or in their domestic and social customs.

These remarks do not apply, we believe, to the members of the Brahma Samaj in Bengal, the Prarthana Samaj in Bombay, or to the associations connected with them.

E.

MOHAMMADAN INTEMPERANCE.

We find a French missionary in Tunis writing thus : " The most shameless drunkenness reigns among all classes in Musalman society. Drunkenness is one of the greatest obstacles we have to contend with in our work among them" (*L'Eglise Libre*, 2 Mai 1888). Unhappily the same thing is true of Mohammadans in many other places.

F.

CREEDS AND CONFESSIONS IN MISSION CHURCHES.

This subject will necessarily require earnest consideration on the part of the Mission Churches. It is interesting to note what is proposed as the doctrinal basis in the contemplated union of Presbyterian and Congregationalist Churches in Japan. All ministers of religion will be required "to accept and subscribe the Apostles' Creed, the Nicene Creed, and the Nine Articles of the Evangelical Alliance." They must also approve of the Westminster Shorter Catechism, the Heidelberg Catechism, and the Plymouth Declaration, "for substance of doctrine." But overtures towards union will be gladly received from other Churches if they can accept as their doctrinal basis the three first-mentioned documents, viz., the Apostles' Creed, the Nicene Creed, and the Nine Articles of the Evangelical Alliance. Certainly a very comprehensive union could be formed on the basis of these three documents.

G.

Comparative Progress of Religions in India.

Since the preceding pages were in type, a lecture on the religions of India has been delivered by Sir W. W. Hunter, who is a high authority on Indian statistics generally. We are happy to see that his conclusions on this much-debated question in no way conflict with the views we have expressed; and we trust his careful statement will put an end to the controversy. Sir William says that, taking Bengal, as being the greatest province outside the famine area of 1877, with a population amounting to one-third of the whole of that of British India, the increase during the nine years preceding 1881 was as follows:—

General population	10.89 per cent.
Mohammadans	10.96 ,,
Hindus, below	13.64 ,,
Native Christians	64.07 ,,

In British India as a whole, so far as statistics are available, the rate was—

Increase of general population	8 per cent.
Increase of Christian population	30 ,,

These are eloquent figures.

INDEX.

Abyssinians, 10.
Academy, Berlin, 99.
Africa, Gospel in North, 46.
African Lakes Company, 60.
Ahriman, 34.
Aitchison, Sir Charles, quoted, 24.
Alighar, Mohammadan education at, 50.
American Board of Commissioners for Foreign Missions, 7.
American *Missionary Herald*, quoted, 23.
American students, awakening among, 90.
Animism, 32.
Appeal to Church, 93.
Arabia, Gospel in, 45.
Armenians, 10.
Arnold, Sir Edwin, 27.
Arthington, Mr., plan of, 85.
Arya Samaj, 27, 43.
Attacks on heathenism to be avoided in preaching, 64.
Authorship, native Christian, 66.

Baba Padmanji, Rev., his works, 29.
Babis in Persia, 44.
Bangor in Wales, 5.
Baptist Missionary Society founded, 6.
Baxter, quoted, 97.
Beck of Tübingen, 8.
Bedell, Bishop, 97.
Beecher Stowe, Mrs., 57.
Benson, Archbishop, quoted, 11.
Berkeley, Bishop, 97.
Bible, missionary spirit in, 1.
Blyden, Dr., quoted, 55.
Bosworth Smith, quoted, 53.

INDEX. 109

Boyle, Hon. Robert, 97.
Brahma Samaj, 43.
Brainerd, 18, 102.
Brassey, Lord, quoted, 57.
Buchanan, Dr. Claudius, 10.
Buddhism, 35; compared with Christianity, 36; missionary zeal of, 80; in Ceylon, 39.
Bulgarians, 10.
Burckhardt, quoted, 54.
Burnouf, quoted, 43.

CANADA Presbyterian Church, mission of, 39
Carey, William, 6.
Celtic missionaries, 4.
Ceylon, Buddhism in, 40.
Character of converts, 18.
Charges against converts, 21.
Children, teaching Gospel to heathen, 66; how to instruct in mission-work, 77.
China Inland Mission, 90.
China, progress of civilisation in, 38; Christianity in, 38; declaration of Government with regard to Christianity, 38.
Chosroes II., 34.
Christian Vernacular Education Society, 66.
Church government, 72.
Church Missionary Society founded, 7; Report quoted, 82.
Churches, appeal to, 93.
Colleges, Christian, 68.
Columba, 4.
Commerce, services rendered by missionaries to, 29.
Comparison of converts with European Christians, 12; Hinduism and Christianity, 20; Buddhism and Christianity, 20.
Conferences, missionary, 84; in the field, 84; at home, 84.
Co-operation in Christian mission-work, 81.
Copts, 10.
Corporation for promoting and propagating the Gospel in New England, 98.
Creeds and conferences in Mission Churches, 106.
Crime in India, statistics of, 19.
Cromwell's plan of propaganda, 97.
Crowther, Bishop, 58.
Cymric (or Welsh) missionaries, 5.

DANISH Mission in Tranquebar, 100.
Darwin, Charles, quoted, 8.
Deputations from Europe, value of, 71.
Despatch, Government, on education, 1854, 67.

Dogmatic teaching, charge of excessive, 67.
Douglas, Frederick, 58.
Duff, Dr., 67, 87.
Dufferin, Countess of, her fund, 70.
Dutch authorities in the East, 52.
Dutch East India Company, 95.
Dutt, Toru, 66.
Dwight, 10.

EARLY Church, missionary spirit in, 1.
East India Company, 98.
Eastern Churches, work among, 3.
Education, higher, 67 ; secular, 67.
Educated Hindus, present state of, 105.
Edwards, Jonathan, treatise of, 103.
Effects of various modes of operation compared, 62.
Egede, Hans, 18, 101.
Egypt, Gospel in, 46.
Eliot, John, 96.
Emin Pasha, quoted, 57.
Endowment of Christian colleges, 68.
English Presbyterian Church, mission of, 39, 82.
Enlargement of effort, necessity of, 68.
Erasmus, 6.

FEMALE Medical Missions, 70.
Ferazi Mohammadans, 48.
Fergusson, Bishop, 59.
First Protestant mission, 95.
Fisk, Pliny, 10.
Formosa, missions in, 39.
Foundation of missionary societies, 6.
Free Church Mission in Arabia, 45.

GIBBON, quoted, 3.
Gilbert, Sir Humphrey, 96.
Gobat, Bishop, 10.
Goodall, 10.
Gordon, Hon. J. H. H., 79.
Gordon Memorial Mission, 80.
Government of Native Churches, forms of, 72.
Grotius, his interest in missions, 97.
Gundert, Dr., quoted, 52.
Gustavus Vasa, 95.

HAIG, General, 45.
Hallam, quoted, 54.

INDEX.

Hatti Humayoon of 1856, 47.
Heber, Bishop, 40.
Herald, Missionary, quoted, 92.
Herbert, George, quoted, 65.
Heyling, Peter, 98.
Hinduism, 40 ; comparison with Christianity, 41.
Holland, 95.
Holly, Bishop, 59.

IGNORANCE concerning missions, 76.
Income, inadequacy of, percentage of, 74.
Increase of Pagan populations, 13.
India, progress of Christianity in, 47.
Indian Archipelago, Christianity in, 51 ; Mohammadanism in, 51 ; encouragement of Christianity by Government in, 52.
Industrial operations in connection with missions, 61.
Influence, "unofficial," 62.
Intellectual standard of Native Christians in India, 20.
Intemperance, Mohammadan, 106.
Intercourse, private, means of conversion, 62.
Interest in missions, chief means of increasing, 76 ; in England, 96.
Iona, 4.
Isaac Taylor, Canon, 52.
Israel, prophets of, 1.

JACOBITE Syrians, 10.
Japan, progress in, 35, 44 ; Christian union in, 82.
Jews, missions to, 9.
Jex-Blake, Dr., quoted, 76.
Johnson, Dr., quoted, 5.
Jowett, Rev. W., 10.
Judson, Dr., quoted, 92.

KAJARNAK, conversion of, 101.
Karens, 26.
Keble, quoted, 84.
Keith-Falconer, Hon. Ion, 45, 79.
Khasias, 41.
Kols, 41.
Koran, 51.
Kugler, Missionary, 10.

LAMARTINE, quoted, 47.
Lander, 55.
Lapland, mission in, 95.
Leibnitz, missionary zeal of, 99.

INDEX.

Leupolt, quoted, 22.
Liberia, 59.
Lichtenstein, Rabbi, 9.
"Light of Asia," Arnold's, 27.
Liquor traffic with the Negroes, 59.
Literary work as a mode of missionary action, 65.
Livingstone, quoted, 53.
London Missionary Society founded, 6.
Lowe, Mr. John, quoted, 61.
Lull, Raymond, 79.
Lütkens, Dr., 100.
Lyall, Sir Arthur, quoted, 48.

MacIvor, Rev. D., quoted, 63.
Mackenzie, Bishop, 18.
Madagascar, martyrs in, 22.
Madras Weekly Mail quoted, 25.
Mahendo, Prince, 80.
Malabar, progress of Mohammadanism in, 49.
Malike, King, appeal of, 59.
Marshman, Dr., quoted, 93.
Martyrs, native, 22.
Massachusetts Company, 96.
Mayhews, the, 96.
May meetings, 77.
M'Cosh, Dr., quoted, 91.
Medical missions, 62, 69.
Mildmay Conference Report, quoted, 46.
Milton, quoted, 22, 94.
Moravians, 39, 101.
Modes of missionary action, 61.
Moffat, Dr., quoted, 29.
Mohammadanism, 43 ; supposed numerical progress in India of, 47 ; declining influence in India of, 49 ; progress in Malabar of, 49 ; number of converts from, 50 ; protection by the Dutch Government of, 52 ; extension in Dutch Indies of, 52 ; extension in Africa of, 52 ; missionaries of, 54 ; vices fostered by, 56 ; overthrows the foundation of Christianity, 53.
Molucca islands, 52.
Moody, Mr., 89.
Moplahs, 49.
Mutiny, Indian, 21.

Negro races, 52 ; capacity of, 57 ; conversions to Mohammadanism of, 52 ; conversions to Christianity of, 57 ; appreciation by missionaries of, 57 ; liquor traffic with, 59 ; worthies, 58.
Nestorian Christians, 3.

INDEX.

Netherlands missionary Society founded, 6.
Nevius, Dr., 62.
Number of Missionary Societies, 7 ; of missionaries, 75.
Numerical results, 13.

OPPOSITION of professed Christians, 7.
Organisation of campaign desirable, 81.

PAGAN religions, state of, 32 ; population, increase of, 13.
Palgrave, W. G., quoted, 55.
Parliament, Long, 96.
Parsis, 33.
Parsons, Levi, 10.
Paulinus of Nola, quoted, 3.
Perkins, Missionary, 10.
Perry, Commodore, 36.
Persia, Gospel in, 44.
Pestalozzi on secular teaching, 67.
Philosophies, Indian, 43.
Plütschau, 100.
Pococke's Arabic translation of treatise by Grotius, 97.
Prayer, season of universal, 85.
Preaching as means of exciting interest in mission-work, 64 ; as mode of missionary action, 62.
Proportion of Christians and Heathen in the world, 12.
Proportional increase of Christians and Heathen in the world, 13.
Promise to Abraham, 1.

QUARTERLY *Review*, 7.

RABINOWICH, Joseph, 9.
Ranade, Hon. G. R., quoted, 26.
Reformers, want of zeal in, reasons for, 5.
Religions in India, comparative progress of, 107.
Repression of Christian effort in Turkey, 46.
Robert College, 10.
Romanists, missions among, 11.

SALAR JUNG, Sir, quoted, 76.
Sanghamitta, Princess, 80.
Santals, 41.
Scandinavia, 99.
Schaff's Encyclopædia, quoted, 5, 100.
Schools as mode of missionary action, 66.
Schreiber, Dr., 52.
Schweinfurth, Dr., 55.

Science, services rendered by missionaries to, 29.
Scottish Missionary Society founded, 6.
Scriptures, circulation of, as means of missionary action, 63.
Secular education in India, 67.
Selim Effendi, convert, 46.
Selwyn, Bishop, 18.
Shairp, Principal, quoted, 79.
Shamanism, 35.
Shiah system of Islam, 44.
Shinshiu sect, statement of a leader of the, 28.
Shintoism, 35.
Singing, influence of, 65.
Smith, Sydney, quoted, 8.
Smith, Eli, Missionary, 10.
Social intercourse, most effective mode of missionary action, 62.
Societies founded, 6; noticed, 98.
South American Missionary Society, 9.
Spartan mother, 78.
Spread of Christianity in first century, 15.
Spurgeon, Mr., quoted, 76.
Statistics of translation of Holy Scriptures, 28; of missionary societies, 6; of missionaries, 75; of increase of population of the world, 12.
Steere, Bishop, 18.
Stephen, Sir Fitzjames, quoted, 41.
Stevenson's, Dr. F., work on missions, 100.
Students, missionary zeal of, 90.
Sufiism in Persia, 44.
Sultan of Turkey, 47.
Sunday-schools, exciting zeal for mission-work in, 77.
Sunni system of Islam, 44.
Syed Ahmed, Sir, 50
Sympathy of converts with other missions, 85.
Syrian Christians of Southern India, 3.

TEACHERS, native, 69.
Tibet, Moravian missions in, 39.
Tiele, Professor, quoted, 32.
Tierra del Fuego, influence of missions in, 9.
Thomas, St., 3.
Tolerance, increase in India of, 24.
Toru Dutt, 66.
Toussaint L'Ouverture, 58.
Tranquebar, Danish mission in, 100.
Translations as a means of missionary action, 65.
Travancore, opinion on secular education of First Prince of, 67; religious teaching in Government school of, 69.

INDEX.

Trivandrum, Government school at, 69.
Turkey, Gospel in, 46.

U-GANDA, martyrs of, 83.
Unbaptized, effects on, 23.
"Uncle Tom," 57.
Unsalaried missionaries, 78.
Unity, Christian, 81.
Universities' Mission, English, 78.

VERNACULAR Education Society, Christian, 66.
Voyage of the *Beagle*, quoted, 20.

WAHABI Mohammadans, 44.
Walæus, Professor, 95.
Waller, Rev. Horace, pamphlet on liquor traffic, 59.
Warneck, Dr., quoted, 102.
Welsh missions, 5.
Welz, Ernst von, 99.
Westen, Thomas von, 99.
Wilberforce, William, quoted, 101.
Wilson, Dr. Leighton, quoted, 56.
Women, influence on, 20.
Wordsworth, quoted, 5.

XAVIER, quoted, 75.

ZENANA Medical Missions, 70.
Zend-Avesta, 34.
Ziegenbalg, 18, 100.
Zinzendorf, 101.
Zoroastrianism, 33.

THE END.

PRINTED BY BALLANTYNE, HANSON AND CO.
EDINBURGH AND LONDON.

PUBLISHED BY JAMES NISBET & CO.

BIOGRAPHY OF THE REV. HENRY A. STERN, D.D., for more than Forty Years a Missionary of the London Society for Promoting Christianity among the Jews. By the Rev. ALBERT A. ISAACS, M.A. With Illustrations. Demy 8vo, 9s.

"Mr. Isaacs has laid the Church under an obligation for the loving care with which he has gathered up this most interesting record of the life and work of one of her Saints. A nobler portraiture of a true Christian hero has not crossed our path in the annals of the early or mediæval Church."—*Church Missionary Intelligencer.*

SAMUEL GOBAT, BISHOP OF JERUSALEM: His Life and Work. A Biographical Sketch, drawn chiefly from his own Journals. Translated and Edited by Mrs. PEREIRA. With Portrait and Illustrations. Crown 8vo, 7s. 6d.

"A pattern memoir; short, compact, and full. It throws much light on Scripture by its vivid description of places, persons, customs, &c., and is otherwise very valuable for its amount of interesting and useful information. A standard work on Missions to the Holy Land."—*Christian World.*

MEMOIR OF THE LATE REV. WILLIAM C. BURNS, M.A., Missionary to China. By the late Professor ISLAY BURNS, D.D., Glasgow. With Portrait. Small crown 8vo, 3s. 6d.

"William Burns is one of the few men of modern times who have carried the Christian idea into such active revelation in the life, as would compel, even from the most sceptical, a reluctant consent to the Divine origin of the truths he taught and lived by; and his memoir, written with rare sincerity and simplicity, must long live as a bright specimen of true Christian biography."—*Contemporary Review.*

THE STORY OF COMMANDER ALLEN GARDINER, R.N. With Sketches of Missionary Work in South America. By JOHN W. MARSH, M.A., and the Right Rev. the BISHOP of the FALKLAND ISLANDS. With Portrait and Maps. Crown 8vo, 2s.

MEMORIALS OF JAMES HENDERSON, M.D., F.R.C.S., Edinburgh, Medical Missionary to China. With Portrait. Crown 8vo, 3s. 6d. Cheap Abridged Edition, 16mo, 1s.

MEMOIR OF THE LATE REV. J. J. WEITBRECHT, late Missionary of the C.M.S. in Bengal. Compiled by his WIDOW from his Journal and his Letters. With a Preface by the late Rev. H. VENN, M.A. Crown 8vo, 3s. 6d.

SEED-TIME IN KASHMIR: A Memoir of WILLIAM J. ELMSLIE, M.D., F.R.C.S.E., late Medical Missionary of the C.M.S. in Kashmir. By his WIDOW and Dr. W. BURNS THOMSON, Medical Missionary. Crown 8vo, 4s. 6d. Cheaper Edition, 1s.

A MISSIONARY OF THE APOSTOLIC SCHOOL: Being the Life of Dr. JUDSON, Missionary to Burmah. Revised and Edited by HORATIUS BONAR, D.D. Crown 8vo, 3s. 6d.

THIRTY-EIGHT YEARS' MISSION LIFE IN JAMAICA: A Brief Sketch of the Rev. WARRAND CARLILE, Missionary at Brownsville. By one of his SONS. Small crown 8vo, 3s. 6d.

LONDON: JAMES NISBET & CO., 21 BERNERS STREET, W.

JAMES NISBET & CO.'S NEW WORKS.

GOSPELS OF YESTERDAY: DRUMMOND — SPENCER — ARNOLD. By ROBERT A. WATSON, M.A. Crown 8vo, 5s.

THE MENTAL CHARACTERISTICS OF OUR LORD JESUS CHRIST. By the Rev. H. N. BERNARD, M.A. Extra crown 8vo, 6s.

THOUGHTS FOR CHURCH SEASONS: In the Order of the Book of Common Prayer. By the Rev. DANIEL MOORE, M.A., Prebendary of St. Paul's, Vicar of Holy Trinity, Paddington, &c. Crown 8vo, 5s.

RIPPLES IN THE MOONLIGHT: Additional Fragments of Sunday Thought and Teaching. By the Rev. J. R. MACDUFF, D.D., Author of "Ripples in the Twilight," &c. Small crown 8vo, 2s.

HOLY IN CHRIST: Thoughts on the Calling of God's Children to be Holy as He is Holy. By the Rev. ANDREW MURRAY, Author of "Abide in Christ," &c. Small crown 8vo, 2s. 6d.

ST. PAUL IN ATHENS: The City and the Discourse. By the Rev. J. R. MACDUFF, D.D. With Illustrations. Crown 8vo, 3s. 6d.

"A thoughtful and beautiful work."—*Sunday School Chronicle.*
"There is much that is attractive in this book."—*Literary Churchman.*

CHRISTIANITY AND EVOLUTION: Modern Problems of the Faith. By the Revs. G. MATHESON, D.D., T. FOWLE, M.A., Sir GEORGE W. COX, M.A., Professor MOMERIE, LL.D., and others. Extra crown 8vo, 6s.

THE FIRST LETTER OF PAUL THE APOSTLE TO TIMOTHY. A Popular Commentary. With a Series of Forty Sermonettes. By ALFRED ROWLAND, LL.B., B.A. (Lond.) Crown 8vo, 6s.

NON-BIBLICAL SYSTEMS OF RELIGION. By the Ven. F. W. FARRAR, D.D., Archdeacon of Westminster, Canon RAWLINSON, Rev. W. WRIGHT, D.D., Rabbi G. J. EMANUEL, B.A., Sir WILLIAM MUIR, and others. Extra crown 8vo, 6s.

THE CHRISTIAN FULFILMENTS AND USES OF THE LEVITICAL SIN-OFFERING. By the Rev. HENRY BATCHELOR. Extra crown 8vo, 5s.

THE PHILOSOPHY OF THE NEW BIRTH. By JOHN EDWIN BRIGG, Vicar of Hepworth, near Huddersfield. Crown 8vo, 2s. 6d.

LONDON: JAMES NISBET & CO., 21 BERNERS STREET, W.

www.ingramcontent.com/pod-product-compliance
Lightning Source LLC
Chambersburg PA
CBHW022140160426
43197CB00009B/1366